Reading Peak 3

NE_Build & Grow

Unit Components

Student Book

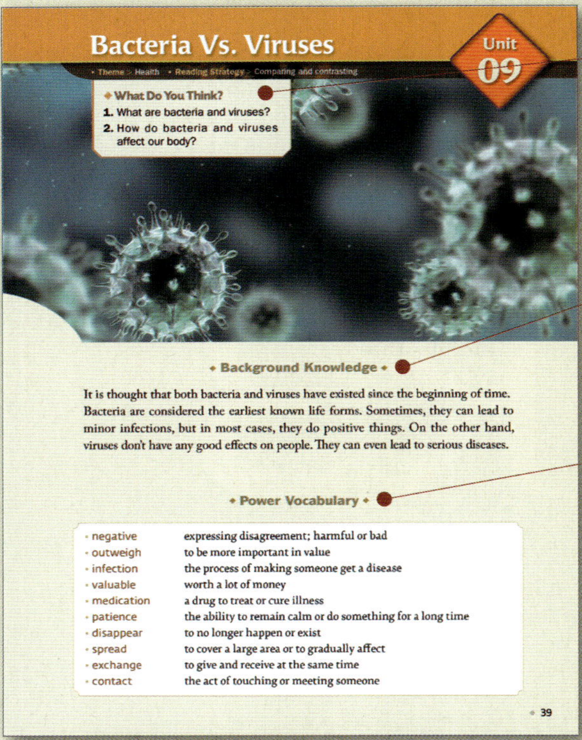

Bacteria Vs. Viruses

Unit 09

• Theme > Health • Reading Strategy > Comparing and contrasting

◆ What Do You Think?

1. What are bacteria and viruses?
2. How do bacteria and viruses affect our body?

◆ Background Knowledge ◆

It is thought that both bacteria and viruses have existed since the beginning of time. Bacteria are considered the earliest known life forms. Sometimes, they can lead to minor infections, but in most cases, they do positive things. On the other hand, viruses don't have any good effects on people. They can even lead to serious diseases.

◆ Power Vocabulary ◆

negative	expressing disagreement; harmful or bad
outweigh	to be more important in value
infection	the process of making someone get a disease
valuable	worth a lot of money
medication	a drug to treat or cure illness
patience	the ability to remain calm or do something for a long time
disappear	to no longer happen or exist
spread	to cover a large area or to gradually affect
exchange	to give and receive at the same time
contact	the act of touching or meeting someone

39

What Do You Think?

Simple warm up questions and related images stimulate students' interest in each topic.

Background Knowledge

Background information is presented to better prepare students for the main readings.

Power Vocabulary

Key words from the main reading passage are carefully chosen and defined to build up students' understanding of the context.

Reading Comprehension

Multiple-choice and short-answer questions are introduced to ensure the students' understanding of the passages.

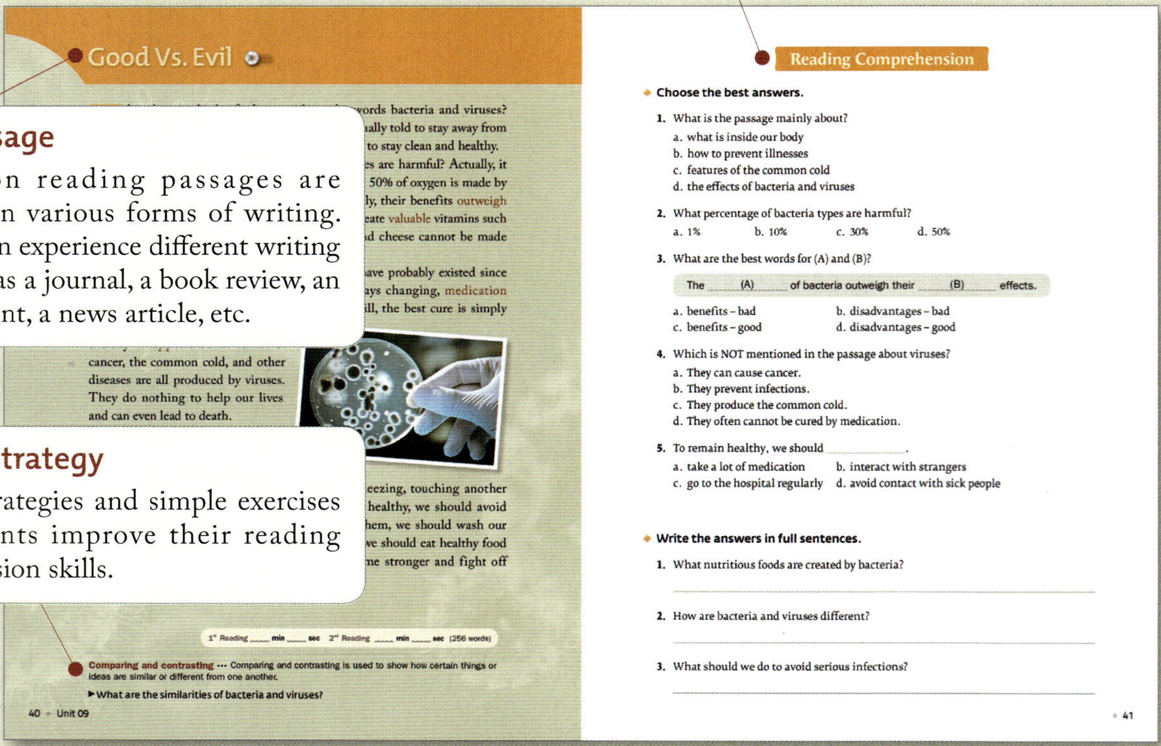

Good Vs. Evil

...words bacteria and viruses? ...ally told to stay away from ... to stay clean and healthy. ...es are harmful? Actually, it ... 50% of oxygen is made by ...ly, their benefits outweigh ...eate valuable vitamins such ...d cheese cannot be made

...ave probably existed since ...ays changing, medication ...ill, the best cure is simply

... cancer, the common cold, and other diseases are all produced by viruses. They do nothing to help our lives and can even lead to death.

...eezing, touching another ... healthy, we should avoid ...hem, we should wash our ...ve should eat healthy food ...me stronger and fight off

1st Reading ___ min ___ sec 2nd Reading ___ min ___ sec (256 words)

Comparing and contrasting ··· Comparing and contrasting is used to show how certain things or ideas are similar or different from one another.

▶ What are the similarities of bacteria and viruses?

40 • Unit 09

Reading Comprehension

◆ Choose the best answers.

1. What is the passage mainly about?
   a. what is inside our body
   b. how to prevent illnesses
   c. features of the common cold
   d. the effects of bacteria and viruses
2. What percentage of bacteria types are harmful?
   a. 1% b. 10% c. 30% d. 50%
3. What are the best words for (A) and (B)?
   The ___(A)___ of bacteria outweigh their ___(B)___ effects.
   a. benefits – bad b. disadvantages – bad
   c. benefits – good d. disadvantages – good
4. Which is NOT mentioned in the passage about viruses?
   a. They can cause cancer.
   b. They prevent infections.
   c. They produce the common cold.
   d. They often cannot be cured by medication.
5. To remain healthy, we should ___________.
   a. take a lot of medication b. interact with strangers
   c. go to the hospital regularly d. avoid contact with sick people

◆ Write the answers in full sentences.

1. What nutritious foods are created by bacteria?
2. How are bacteria and viruses different?
3. What should we do to avoid serious infections?

41

Main Passage

Nonfiction reading passages are presented in various forms of writing. Students can experience different writing styles such as a journal, a book review, an advertisement, a news article, etc.

Reading Strategy

Reading strategies and simple exercises help students improve their reading comprehension skills.

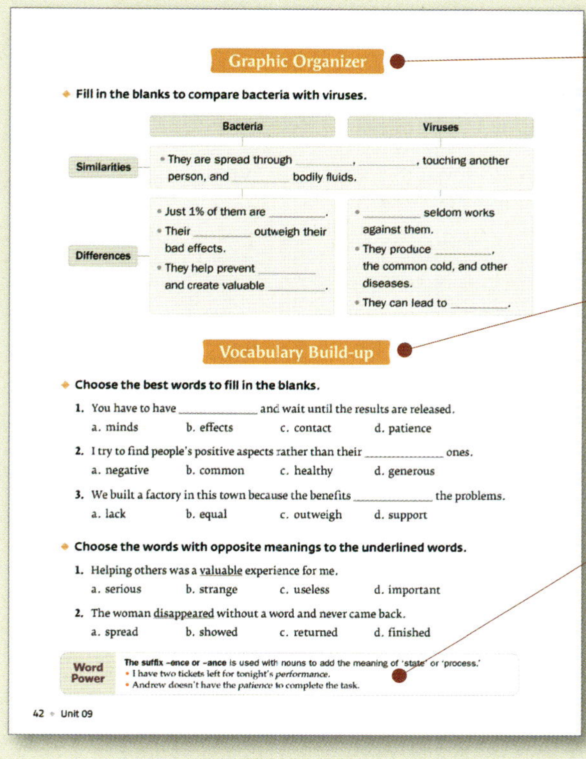
Graphic Organizer

◆ Fill in the blanks to compare bacteria with viruses.

	Bacteria	Viruses
Similarities	• They are spread through _______, _______, touching another person, and _______ bodily fluids.	
Differences	• Just 1% of them are _______. • Their _______ outweigh their bad effects. • They help prevent _______ and create valuable _______.	• _______ seldom works against them. • They produce _______, the common cold, and other diseases. • They can lead to _______.

Vocabulary Build-up

◆ Choose the best words to fill in the blanks.

1. You have to have _______ and wait until the results are released.
   a. minds b. effects c. contact d. patience
2. I try to find people's positive aspects rather than their _______ ones.
   a. negative b. common c. healthy d. generous
3. We built a factory in this town because the benefits _______ the problems.
   a. lack b. equal c. outweigh d. support

◆ Choose the words with opposite meanings to the underlined words.

1. Helping others was a valuable experience for me.
   a. serious b. strange c. useless d. important
2. The woman disappeared without a word and never came back.
   a. spread b. showed c. returned d. finished

Word Power The suffix -ence or -ance is used with nouns to add the meaning of 'state' or 'process.'
• I have two tickets left for tonight's *performance*.
• Andrew doesn't have the *patience* to complete the task.

42 • Unit 09

Graphic Organizer

Graphic organizers help students summarize the information from the main reading passages logically.

Vocabulary Build-up

Additional multiple-choice questions further strengthen students' vocabulary acquisition.

Word Power

The uses of different prefixes, suffixes, and root words are explained with more examples.

Writing Practice

Grammar and writing practice enhance students' writing skills.

Workbook

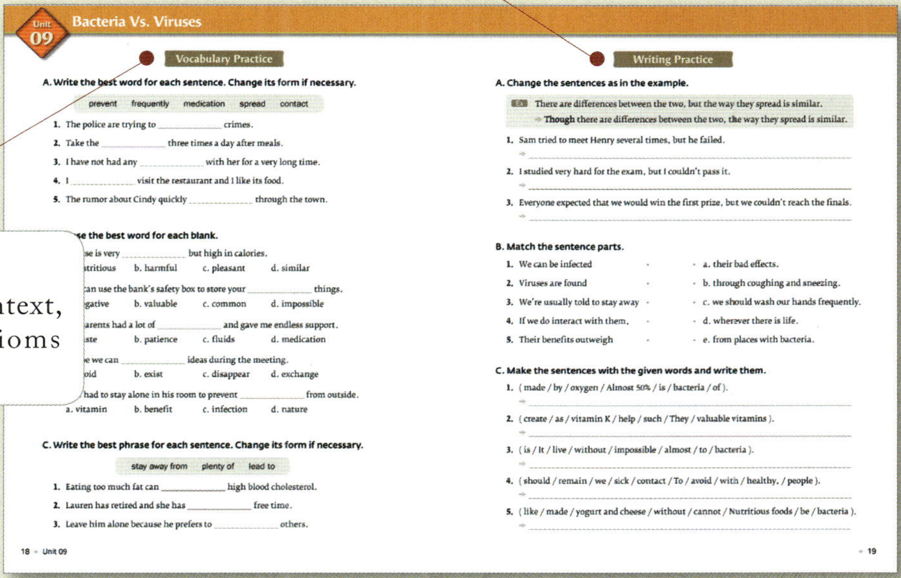
Unit 09 Bacteria Vs. Viruses

Vocabulary Practice

A. Write the best word for each sentence. Change its form if necessary.

prevent frequently medication spread contact

1. The police are trying to _______ crimes.
2. Take the _______ three times a day after meals.
3. I have not had any _______ with her for a very long time.
4. I _______ visit the restaurant and I like its food.
5. The rumor about Cindy quickly _______ through the town.

...se the best word for each blank.

...se is very _______ but high in calories.
...tritious b. harmful c. pleasant d. similar
...an use the bank's safety box to store your _______ things.
...gative b. valuable c. common d. impossible
...arents had a lot of _______ and gave me endless support.
...ste b. patience c. fluids d. medication
...e we can _______ ideas during the meeting.
...oid b. exist c. disappear d. exchange
... had to stay alone in his room to prevent _______ from outside.
a. vitamin b. benefit c. infection d. nature

C. Write the best phrase for each sentence. Change its form if necessary.

stay away from plenty of lead to

1. Eating too much fat can _______ high blood cholesterol.
2. Lauren has retired and she has _______ free time.
3. Leave him alone because he prefers to _______ others.

18 • Unit 09

Writing Practice

A. Change the sentences as in the example.

Ex There are differences between the two, but the way they spread is similar.
→ **Though** there are differences between the two, the way they spread is similar.

1. Sam tried to meet Henry several times, but he failed.
   → _______
2. I studied very hard for the exam, but I couldn't pass it.
   → _______
3. Everyone expected that we would win the first prize, but we couldn't reach the finals.
   → _______

B. Match the sentence parts.

1. We can be infected • • a. their bad effects.
2. Viruses are found • • b. through coughing and sneezing.
3. We're usually told to stay away • • c. we should wash our hands frequently.
4. If we do interact with them, • • d. wherever there is life.
5. Their benefits outweigh • • e. from places with bacteria.

C. Make the sentences with the given words and write them.

1. (made / by / oxygen / Almost 50% / is / bacteria / of).
   → _______
2. (create / as / vitamin K / help / such / They / valuable vitamins).
   → _______
3. (is / It / live / without / impossible / almost / to / bacteria).
   → _______
4. (should / remain / we / sick / contact / To / avoid / with / healthy, / people).
   → _______
5. (like / made / yogurt and cheese / without / cannot / Nutritious foods / be / bacteria).
   → _______

• 19

Vocabulary Practice

Exercises on new words in context, synonyms, antonyms, and idioms improve students' vocabulary.

Scope and Sequence

A Fairy Tale

Unit 01

• Theme > Tales • Reading Strategy > Drawing conclusions

◆ What Do You Think?

1. What is a fairy tale?

2. What is your favorite fairy tale and why?

◆ Background Knowledge ◆

Don't be confused by the name "fairy tale": Only a few "fairy tales" are actually about fairies. The word is used for folk stories, usually for children. These stories include magic or imaginary beings like dragons or giants. Generally, fairy tales do not seem real. They are stories about events that could never happen, and they allow us to imagine a whole new world.

◆ Power Vocabulary ◆

• original	the first made or performed
• violent	acting with great force or anger
• scholar	someone with great knowledge, usually acquired from research
• folk	traditional; typical of a community or nation
• publish	to put into print
• religious	concerned with religion or the church
• scary	causing fear or alarm
• translate	to change words from one language into another language
• nightmare	a deeply upsetting dream
• frightening	causing fear or terror

Stories before Bedtime

Do you know the story of "Little Red Riding Hood"? In the story, a little girl goes into the forest to visit her sick grandmother, and a wolf catches her. Does it sound scary? Well, the original story was even more violent. It was first written in the 1800s by two brothers, Jacob and Wilhelm Grimm. In their version, after the wolf eats the grandmother and the little girl, a hunter saves them by cutting open the wolf's stomach with scissors!

The Brothers Grimm were German scholars. They wanted to introduce German culture through their stories. They asked many German people about German folk stories. Then, they wrote these stories down and published them. Their fairy tales were more religious and included less magic than other fairy tales. In fact, some of them didn't have any magic. They were also famous because they were very violent and scary. Still, people around the world have read their stories and translated them into more than 160 languages.

The stories of the Brothers Grimm are still enjoyed around the world today, but people have changed them so that they can be told to children. For example, in the Brothers Grimm version of "Sleeping Beauty," the fairy Maleficent was an ogre[1] who wanted to eat Sleeping Beauty. However, the Disney movie *Sleeping Beauty* changed this character to be less scary.

Many children read these stories before going to sleep, and their parents don't want their kids to have nightmares. That's why fairy tales today are usually not too frightening, and they always have a happy ending.

1 ogre: an imaginary ugly giant that eats people

1st Reading _____ min _____ sec 2nd Reading _____ min _____ sec (264 words)

Drawing conclusions ··· To draw a conclusion, you need to consider all the clues and facts presented in a given text.

▶ What conclusion did you draw from the passage?

Reading Comprehension

Choose the best answers.

1. What is the passage mainly about?

a. fairy tales for adults b. the Brothers Grimm fairy tales
c. the features of fairy tales d. the different kinds of fairy tales

2. Which is NOT true according to the passage?

a. The Brothers Grimm were German scholars.
b. The Brothers Grimm used German folk stories for their fairy tales.
c. "Little Red Riding Hood" was first written by the Brothers Grimm.
d. The Brothers Grimm tales couldn't be translated into other languages.

3. The Brothers Grimm tales are famous for being very ______________.

a. magical b. violent c. sorrowful d. interesting

4. What are the best words for (A) and (B)?

The Grimm fairy tales are ____(A)____ religious and ____(B)____ magical than other fairy tales.

a. less – more b. more – less
c. more – least d. least – most

5. Why do fairy tales today always have a happy ending?

a. It allows people to be more religious.
b. It allows children to fall asleep quicker.
c. It allows children not to have nightmares.
d. It allows Germans to feel more proud of them.

Write the answers in full sentences.

1. When was "Little Red Riding Hood" first written?

____

2. What did the Brothers Grimm want to introduce in their fairy tales?

____

3. What was the fairy Maleficent in the Brothers Grimm version of "Sleeping Beauty"?

____

Graphic Organizer

◆ **Fill in the blanks to explain the differences between the original Brothers Grimm stories and the changed versions.**

The Original Versions of the Brothers Grimm Stories	Changed Versions of the Brothers Grimm Stories
• introduce German culture • are based on German ________ stories • were more ________ and included less magic • were very violent and ________	• are changed to be appropriate for ________ • are less ________ • have a(n) ________ ending

Vocabulary Build-up

◆ **Choose the best words to fill in the blanks.**

1. Jack wants to ____________ the stories he has written.

a. cause b. scare c. publish d. interview

2. Millions of people came to America for ____________ freedom.

a. happy b. magic c. religious d. violent

3. The ____________ version of the novel is different from this one.

a. evil b. ending c. constant d. original

◆ **Choose the words with similar meanings to the underlined words.**

1. The story developed from folk beliefs.

a. unique b. practical c. incredible d. traditional

2. The last scene of the movie is very frightening.

a. scary b. famous c. popular d. exciting

Word Power

The suffix –ous is added to adjectives to produce the meaning of 'possessing' or 'full of.'

- There have been many *religious* wars in the world.
- I don't have any *serious* problems with my health.

Fair Trade

Unit 02

• **Theme** > Economy • **Reading Strategy** > Distinguishing fact from opinion

◆ What Do You Think?

1. What is fair trade?
2. Do you think our economy is run fairly?

◆ Background Knowledge ◆

The fair trade movement insists that regular trade should change because it is unfair to workers in poorer parts of the world. Labor is generally cheaper in poor regions, but when products are sold in wealthy countries, the price increases. That extra money usually doesn't go to the workers, but to the sellers. With fair trade products, most of the extra money goes to the workers.

◆ Power Vocabulary ◆

• fair	based on moral and just decisions
• opinion	someone's belief or idea
• average	the typical amount, quality, degree, etc.
• afford	to be able to pay for something
• extra	more than what is usual or necessary
• involve	to take in or gather in
• earn	to get by efforts
• additional	often more than expected
• encourage	to give hope or confidence
• rare	not well-known; not many

Is Fair Trade Really Fair? T02

Debate

Presenter: Hi, folks. Today we're talking to Ashley Wilson who always buys fair trade products, and Sean Davis, an economist. Let's hear their opinions.

Ashley: We all know the average American makes more money than the average Tanzanian does. With fair trade, we can purchase Tanzanian goods[1] for a fairer price. By paying a little more for these products, we can afford to pay workers with the extra money. When trading goods, there are usually extra companies, or middlemen, involved who must be paid. Since there are no middlemen in fair trade, there is more money for the workers. Also fair trade makes sure that workers earn a good salary in a safe workplace. Like other fair trade product users, I want to make a difference in the lives of poor people. Fair trade is a good start for sure.

Sean: I agree that workers should be paid a fair price. But there are also some serious problems with fair trade. Stores know that people will pay more for fair trade items, so they raise the prices. Then they keep this additional money instead of giving it to the workers. Another problem is that fair trade encourages workers to make more of certain items. Since they know they can sell these items for a good price, the workers make too many of them. This causes a problem. If there is too much of a product, the price goes down. This happens because it isn't rare anymore. So fair trade doesn't work in the long run.

Presenter: Now, audience, it's up to you. What do you think?

1 goods: items or products

1st Reading ____ min ____ sec 2nd Reading ____ min ____ sec (266 words)

Distinguishing fact from opinion ··· A fact is something that is either true or untrue and which can be proved. An opinion is a person's own view, judgment, or attitude. It can be distinguished by 'I think,' 'I believe,' or 'in my opinion.'

► What is Ashley's opinion about fair trade?

Reading Comprehension

Choose the best answers.

1. What is the passage mainly about?

a. a debate on fair trade
b. the important roles of trade
c. the bad effects of fair trade
d. the average Tanzanian income

2. Which is NOT true according to the passage?

a. Stores raise the prices of fair trade items.
b. There are middlemen involved in trading goods.
c. Sean thinks that workers keep the additional money.
d. The average American makes more money than the average Tanzanian.

3. Why does the price go down if there is too much of a product?

a. because the product isn't rare anymore
b. because it is difficult to buy the product
c. because no one needs the product anymore
d. because the product is not in a good condition

4. Ashley thinks fair trade helps workers earn a ______________ salary.

a. bad b. low c. good d. safe

5. What do both Ashley and Sean agree on?

a. Workers should be paid a fair price.
b. Fair trade will work in the long run.
c. Fair trade is not good for poor people.
d. There is no problem with fair trade at all.

Write the answers in full sentences.

1. What does Ashley want to make a difference in?

____

2. According to Sean, where does the money from fair trade go to?

____

3. Who does Sean think fair trade workers make more of certain items?

____

Graphic Organizer

◆ **Fill in the blanks based on two opinions about fair trade.**

Fair Trade

Pros

- The average American makes __________ money than the average Tanzanian.
- There are no middlemen in fair tade, so there is more money for the workers.
- Workers earn a good __________ in a safe workplace.

Cons

- Workers are encouraged to __________ more of certain items, which will make their price go __________.
- Stores keep the __________ money from fair trade instead of giving it to the workers.

Vocabulary Build-up

◆ **Choose the best words to fill in the blanks.**

1. The two debaters had different ______________ on the subject.

a. grades b. styles c. opinions d. organizations

2. The ______________ age of our workers is around thirty.

a. extra b. excess c. average d. economic

3. Save your money, and you can ______________ to buy what you want.

a. learn b. afford c. discover d. accomplish

◆ **Choose the words with similar meanings to the underlined words.**

1. The teacher tried to <u>encourage</u> the boy's musical talents.

a. hide b. worry c. reject d. inspire

2. Alicia believed the judgment was not <u>fair</u>, so she complained to the judge.

a. just b. true c. firm d. wrong

Word Power

The prefix en– is used to add the meaning of 'to make' or 'to put within.'

- My parents *encourage* me to do what I want to.
- If you develop this area, you may *endanger* the wildlife.

Claude Monet

Unit 03

• Theme > Art • Reading Strategy > Understanding sequences

What Do You Think?

1. Who is your favorite artist and why?
2. Who was Claude Monet?

Background Knowledge

Claude Monet was a French painter born in 1840. He is known as the father of impressionism. An impression is a feeling or an idea you get from something, so impressionism is a style of painting that is not exactly realistic. Instead, impressionist painters like Monet tried to capture a mood or an emotion in their paintings.

Power Vocabulary

• term	a word or phrase to explain something
• subject	a person, place, or thing discussed about
• exactly	just as it should be
• capture	to clearly show what something is really like
• significance	importance; the special meaning of something
• appearance	visible look of a person or thing
• emotion	a feeling that someone experiences
• pave	to create a situation that makes easier for something to happen
• abstract	not physical; describing something formed in the mind
• freedom	a state of independence

Monet's Garden

Today many people love Claude Monet's first impressionist painting, *Impression, Sunrise*. However, when he first showed it, people laughed at it because it wasn't realistic. At that time, people thought paintings should look like reality. Actually, the term "impressionist" did not originally have a positive meaning. A journalist first used it as a joke. Little did he know it would become the name for a much-loved style of painting!

Monet's early paintings were in the realist style, but later he painted in his own impressionist style. He started to focus on light and color, not people or objects. He would paint one object, like a haystack or the Rouen Cathedral, over and over at different times of the day and in different kinds of weather.

One of Monet's most famous subjects is water lilies. He painted over 250 water lily paintings. Many of them look alike, but no two are exactly the same. He painted them in various colors and types of light. Finally, he was able to capture the way the light changed their appearance. In these paintings, the flowers lose significance and the mood becomes an important feature.

As Monet focused on emotion rather than realism, people were shocked at first. But they soon began to see how light can be beautiful. Other artists like Renoir and Degas began to paint in the impressionist style, and together they paved the way for all kinds of abstract paintings. Thanks to Monet, modern painters have the freedom to paint what they feel, not just what they see.

1st Reading _____ min _____ sec 2nd Reading _____ min _____ sec (257 words)

Understanding sequences ··· Stories are usually told in the order in which the events occurred — from beginning to ending.

► What style were Monet's early paintings?

Reading Comprehension

Choose the best answers.

1. What is the passage mainly about?

a. realistic painters
b. Renoir and Degas
c. kinds of paintings
d. Monet and impressionist painting

2. Which is NOT true according to the passage?

a. Monet's early paintings were in the realistic style.
b. One of Monet's most famous subjects is water lilies.
c. People liked Monet's first impressionist painting at first.
d. Monet used to paint one object over and over at different times.

3. Monet focused on light and color instead of ______________ in his later paintings.

a. freedom　　b. weather
c. abstract things　　d. people and objects

4. What is important in the impressionist style?

a. tools　　b. price
c. mood　　d. objects

5. Who later started to paint in the impressionist style as well?

a. Dali　　b. Renoir
c. Picasso　　d. da Vinci

Write the answers in full sentences.

1. How did the term "impressionist" start?

____

2. Before impressionism, what did people think paintings should look like?

____

3. Why were Monet's paintings of the same objects not all the same?

____

Graphic Organizer

◆ **Fill in the blanks to compare Monet's early paintings with later paintings.**

Monet's Paintings

Early Paintings	Later Paintings
• the __________ style • focused more on __________ or __________	• the __________ style • focused on __________ and __________ • were painted at different __________ of the day and different kinds of __________

Vocabulary Build-up

◆ **Choose the best words to fill in the blanks.**

1. The robot is so ______________ that it is almost like a human.

a. fake b. quiet c. realistic d. artificial

2. The painter expresses his ______________ through his paintings.

a. price b. products c. subjects d. emotions

3. The writer's ideas are very ______________, so I cannot understand them.

a. abstract b. demanding c. impressive d. well-known

◆ **Choose the words with similar meanings to the underlined words.**

1. This building has historical <u>significance</u> to Americans.

a. subject b. author c. opinion d. importance

2. As teenagers grow up, most want to have complete <u>freedom</u>.

a. mood b. type c. feature d. independence

Word Power

The suffix -dom is added to adjectives to produce the meaning of 'place' or 'state of being.'
- *Freedom* of expression is very important.
- The main difference between humans and animals is that humans have *wisdom*.

Shark Fins

Unit 04

• **Theme** > Ecosystem • **Reading Strategy** > Recognizing cause and effect

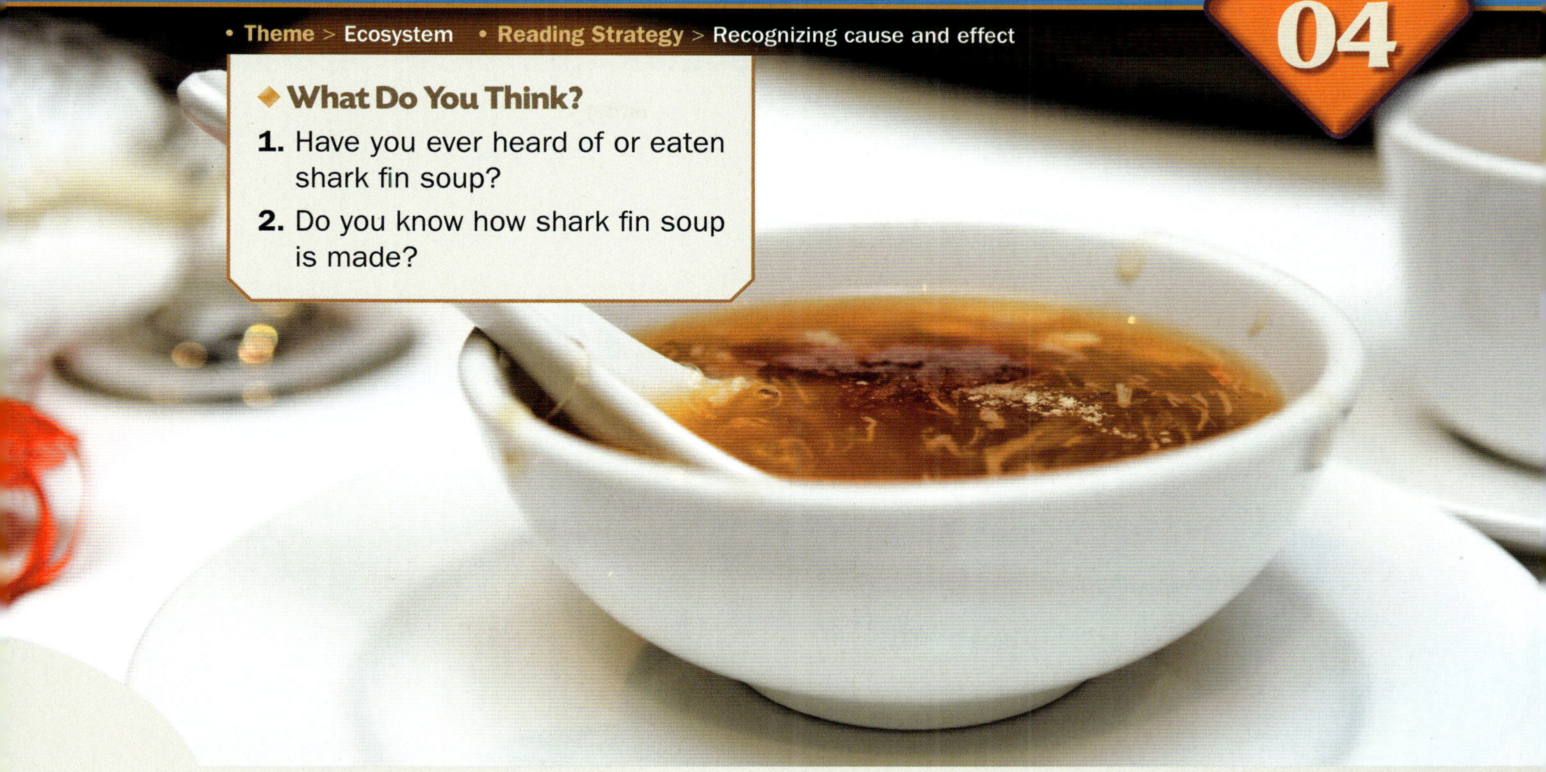

◆ What Do You Think?

1. Have you ever heard of or eaten shark fin soup?
2. Do you know how shark fin soup is made?

◆ Background Knowledge ◆

Our oceans' ecosystems are like a carefully balanced ladder. At the top are the big predators. At the bottom are the plants. This is also called the food chain. Taking away part of the ladder breaks the whole system because each species is dependent on others. Without prey, the predators would not survive. Without the predators, there would be too much prey and they would destroy the ecosystem.

◆ Power Vocabulary ◆

• terrify	to fill with terror
• practice	a way of doing something
• prey	an animal that is caught and eaten by another animal
• demand	the need or desire to buy particular goods or services
• extinction	the death of all living members of a certain species
• official	people in the government
• enforce	to make sure that a law or rule is obeyed by people
• monitor	to observe or record an activity or performance
• ban	to officially say that someone is not allowed to do something
• ingredient	food that is part of a cooking process

A Dangerous Delicacy

T04

Editorial

Many people think of sharks as terrifying animals, so it may surprise you to know that some people eat them. Shark fin soup is a specialty in China, and more and more people are eating it these days.

Shark fin soup uses only the sharks' fins, not any other part. So fishermen usually catch the sharks, cut off their fins, and throw the sharks back into the water. What a cruel and wasteful practice it is! It means that the sharks can no longer swim. Once the rulers of the ocean, they become prey for other fish.

As demand for shark fin soup rises, sharks are increasingly in danger of overfishing and even extinction. This isn't just a problem for the sharks. Since sharks are at the top of the food chain in the ocean, they are very important to the ecosystem's balance. They eat smaller fish, and these fish eat oxygen-producing plants. This oxygen is necessary for human life. Without sharks, there would be too many smaller fish and they would eat all the plants. This would mean less oxygen for humans. The smaller fish would certainly be happy with less predators, but it wouldn't be good for the ecosystem of the ocean.

Officials should at least enforce the fishing laws that are already in place. New international laws should also be created so that countries can work together to monitor shark fishing. Finally, a ban on shark fin soup would decrease demand for sharks' fins. Sharks should be a key ingredient not in soup but in the ecosystem.

1st Reading _____ min _____ sec 2nd Reading _____ min _____ sec (260 words)

Recognizing cause and effect ··· The cause and effect are the reason and the result of an event. The cause makes the effect happen.

▶ Why is the ecosystem of the ocean being destroyed?

Reading Comprehension

◆ Choose the best answers.

1. What is the passage mainly about?

a. the features of ocean animals
b. the ways to cook shark fin soup
c. the reasons why Chinese food is popular
d. the causes and effects of shark overfishing

2. What do fishermen usually do after catching sharks?

a. feed many smaller fish
b. cut them into many parts
c. sell them at the market
d. cut off their fins and release them

3. What do sharks eat?

a. plants
b. humans
c. smaller fish
d. other sharks

4. What are the best words for (A) and (B)?

> As demand for shark fin soup ____(A)____, sharks are ____(B)____ in danger.

a. falls – certainly
b. falls – increasingly
c. rises – decreasingly
d. rises – increasingly

5. Which is NOT an opinion of the writer?

a. All fishing should be made illegal.
b. Laws should ban the eating of shark fin soup.
c. Officials should enforce existing fishing laws.
d. Countries need to work together to monitor shark fishing.

◆ Write the answers in full sentences.

1. Why are sharks an important part of the ecosystem?

____

2. What would happen if there were too many smaller fish?

____

3. Why should new international laws be created?

____

Graphic Organizer

◆ **Fill in the blanks to explain endangered sharks.**

Endangered Sharks

Problems	Solutions
• increasing demand for shark fin ________	• enforcing the present fishing ________
• killing sharks only for their ________	• creating new international laws to ________ shark fishing
• danger of overfishing and ________ of sharks	• a(n) ________ on shark fin soup

Vocabulary Build-up

◆ **Choose the best words to fill in the blanks.**

1. Recycling is an environmentally friendly ____________.

a. predator b. practice c. extinction d. ecosystem

2. All the children were ____________ by the ghost stories.

a. meant b. created c. terrified d. enforced

3. The TV program was ____________ because it was too violent.

a. banned b. allowed c. produced d. increased

◆ **Choose the words with similar meanings to the underlined words.**

1. The actress <u>monitored</u> the editing of the film's script.

a. released b. removed c. decreased d. supervised

2. The workers made a <u>demand</u> for a pay increase.

a. request b. balance c. question d. specialty

Word Power

The suffix –fy is used to produce the meaning of 'make,' 'do,' 'build,' or 'cause.'

• People were *terrified* by the natural disaster.
• The Egyptians *mummified* their pharaohs.

Nomadic People

Unit 05

• **Theme** > Anthropology • **Reading Strategy** > Drawing conclusions

◆ **What Do You Think?**

1. What kind of shelter do you live in?
2. How many times have you moved in your lifetime?

◆ Background Knowledge ◆

The nomadic lifestyle is the oldest human survival method. Nomadic people do not have a permanent home. They travel from place to place during different seasons to escape harsh weather, to hunt animals for food, and to farm new soil. After industrialization began, however, many people moved to cities where they could have a stable lifestyle with a home and a job.

◆ Power Vocabulary ◆

• shelter	a safe place to stay
• consider	to think about something carefully before making a decision
• grassland	a large area of land where wild grass grows
• possession	anything owned
• harsh	unpleasant and difficult
• boil	to pass from a liquid to vapor when heated
• consist	to be made up or composed of
• crop	a plant grown for food, usually on a farm
• outdated	old; no longer fashionable
• respect	to think much of; to regard highly

Home Away from Home

Do you live in a house or an apartment? All around the world, almost everyone lives in some kind of shelter. But there are some people who have special homes. Tibetan nomads travel all the time. They consider the mountains and grasslands of the Tibetan Plateau their home.

As Tibetan nomads travel constantly, they only own important things and take full advantage of them to survive. One of their most important possessions is yaks. Yaks are used for shelter, clothes, and food. Tibetan nomads make tents from yak wool. These tents are light and convenient so the nomads can carry them around easily. Also, yak skin protects them from the harsh weather of the Tibetan Plateau. Dried yak dung is used to cook food and boil water.

The daily diet of Tibetan nomads consists of yak meat, cheese, yogurt, and animals that can be hunted and fished for in local areas. To grow crops, Tibetan nomads use fertile land. They go to another place before the soil turns bad. Once or twice a year, they get together at markets or festivals and trade the things they have, such as crops and animals, for the things they need.

The lifestyle of Tibetan nomads is being threatened by big cities. Many cultures have traditionally been nomadic, but this is rarely seen nowadays. The lifestyle of Tibetan nomads is quite different and may be outdated. But it is important to respect and maintain every way of life in the world. Differences make this world an interesting place to live in.

1st Reading _____ min _____ sec 2nd Reading _____ min _____ sec (257 words)

Drawing conclusions ··· When you draw a conclusion, you need to combine your own knowledge and the information presented in a given text.

▶ What conclusion did you draw from the story?

Reading Comprehension

Choose the best answers.

1. What is the passage mainly about?
   a. various lifestyles
   b. the significance of shelters
   c. the different kinds of shelters
   d. the lifestyle of Tibetan nomads

2. Tibetan nomads consider ______________ of the Tibetan Plateau their home.
   a. big cities　　b. fertile land
   c. an apartment　　d. the mountains and grasslands

3. Which is NOT one of the Tibetan nomads' uses of yaks?
   a. a daily diet of yak meat
   b. tents made from yak wool
   c. yak dung used as a fertilizer
   d. yak skin to protect them from harsh weather

4. Tibetan nomads ______________ for fertile land to grow crops.
   a. use yaks　　b. use advanced machines
   c. use organic fertilizer　　d. move from place to place

5. Which is NOT true according to the passage?
   a. The weather in the Tibetan Plateau is mild.
   b. The lifestyle of Tibetan nomads is being threatened.
   c. Tibetan nomads trade things at markets or festivals.
   d. Tibetan nomads use dried dung to cook food and boil water.

Write the answers in full sentences.

1. Why are yaks the most important possession for Tibetan nomads?

   ____

2. What is the daily diet of Tibetan nomads?

   ____

3. How can Tibetan nomads trade things?

   ____

Graphic Organizer

◆ **Fill in the blanks to explain the lifestyle of Tibetan nomads.**

Tibetan Nomads

Shelter	Clothes	Food
• __________ from yak wool	• yak skin to protect them from __________ weather	• yak meat, cheese, yogurt, animals hunted and fished for in __________ areas • __________ grown on fertile land

Vocabulary Build-up

◆ **Choose the best words to fill in the blanks.**

1. We have to ______________ the rich experiences of our elders.

a. trade b. expect c. respect d. survive

2. Your final exam will ______________ of five essay questions.

a. hunt b. protect c. consist d. consider

3. Almost all the ______________ dried out because of the severe drought.

a. wool b. crops c. shelters d. festivals

◆ **Choose the words with opposite meanings to the underlined words.**

1. Miller always listens to <u>outdated</u> songs.

a. old b. recent c. popular d. fashionable

2. The <u>harsh</u> weather continued for several days.

a. mild b. severe c. tough d. rough

Word Power

The prefix con– is used to add the meaning of 'with,' 'together,' or 'joint.'

- I'd like to *confirm* my reservation by email.
- The city is planning to *construct* the tallest building in the world.

Constellations

Unit 06

• Theme > Astrology • Reading Strategy > Distinguishing real from make-believe

◆ **What Do You Think?**

1. Can you name a constellation?

2. What does the Great Bear look like?

◆ Background Knowledge ◆

Many societies have created stories about the stars and tried to explain how they affect humans. More than 3,000 years ago in ancient Babylon, people tried to understand their lives using star patterns. This was the beginning of astrology: the idea that you can understand your personality and predict future events in your life by studying the movement of the stars.

◆ Power Vocabulary ◆

• enormous	extremely large
• vicious	likely to be cruel or violent
• tough	strong
• courageous	brave; able to manage fear
• realize	to become aware of something
• coward	a person who shows fear or who lacks courage
• escape	to get away; to avoid danger
• pursue	to run after or follow in order to catch
• approach	to get near something
• drip	to fall in drops

The Great Bear in the Sky

In the past, when people were lost in the woods, they often looked for a group of stars called the Big Dipper. This told them which direction was north. But the Big Dipper is actually part of a larger constellation known as Ursa Major, which means "Great Bear" in Latin. It was given this name because the stars form a shape similar to a big bear. Many different cultures have interesting stories about this big bear in the night sky.

One myth about Ursa Major comes from a Native American tribe in Canada called the Algonquin. The story says there was an enormous bear that was very vicious. His favorite pastime was attacking villages and people. Finally, the elders of three different villages decided to pick out their best warriors to hunt the bear. The three warriors were very tough and courageous. When the bear realized they were hunting him, he was so terrified that he ran away. He was certainly scary, but he was also a coward. The warriors chased him for months and months, and he started to get tired. He ran into the sky to escape the warriors, but he didn't expect them to pursue him! They entered the sky with him and chased him around Ursa Major, continuing to circle around it. One day in fall, one of the warriors shot the bear with an arrow. He didn't die, but he began to bleed. So every fall, when the bear approaches the horizon, his blood drips onto the Earth. This causes the trees to turn red and orange!

1st Reading _____ min _____ sec 2nd Reading _____ min _____ sec (263 words)

Distinguishing real from make-believe ··· To distinguish real from make-believe, you need to figure out what can happen in real life and what could not. News reports or biographies are real stories. Fables, science fiction, and mythology are make-believe stories.

▶ What are the make-believe aspects of this story?

Reading Comprehension

◆ Choose the best answers.

1. What is the passage mainly about?

a. space
b. Ursa Major
c. constellations
d. the Algonquin

2. The Big Dipper told people which direction was ______________.

a. east
b. west
c. south
d. north

3. Which is NOT true according to the passage?

a. Ursa Major means Great Bear in Latin.
b. People looked for the Big Dipper when they were lost.
c. Ursa Major is part of the constellation, the Big Dipper.
d. The Algonquin made one of the myths about Ursa Major.

4. What are the best words for (A) and (B)?

> The enormous bear was ______(A)______ but he was also a ______(B)______.

a. shy – hero
b. kind – coward
c. scary – hero
d. vicious – coward

5. What did the three warriors chase the bear around?

a. the sun
b. Ursa Major
c. the arrow
d. the Big Dipper

◆ Write the answers in full sentences.

1. Why was Ursa Major given the name "Great Bear" in Latin?

____

2. According to one myth about Ursa Major, why did the bear run into the sky?

____

3. According to the myth, why do the trees turn red and orange in the fall?

____

Graphic Organizer

◆ **Fill in the blanks to explain one myth about Ursa Major.**

A Myth about Ursa Major

An enormous bear __________ villages and people. Three warriors were chosen to __________ the bear. The bear was so __________ and ran away. The warriors __________ the bear around __________ __________. One day in the fall, the bear was shot by one of the warrior's __________. Every fall, the bear's __________ drips on to the Earth when he approaches the horizon. The trees turn red and orange in the fall.

Vocabulary Build-up

◆ **Choose the best words to fill in the blanks.**

1. Jack is too weak to carry the ______________ bucket up the hill.
a. brown b. small c. light d. enormous

2. I ______________ that I sent the email to the wrong person.
a. realized b. expected c. relieved d. respected

3. Emily is a ______________ so she cannot make decisions easily.
a. hero b. major c. warrior d. coward

◆ **Choose the words with similar meanings to the underlined words.**

1. Tina ran away to <u>escape</u> the dangerous situation.
a. avoid b. expect c. attack d. approach

2. The <u>courageous</u> man saved a little girl from a burning building.
a. weak b. scary c. brave d. terrifying

Word Power

The suffix -ize is used to make verbs and means 'to make.'
- I didn't *realize* how honest he was.
- The brutal crimes *terrorized* the people in this town.

LOHAS

Unit 07

• Theme > Environment • Reading Strategy > Guessing word meaning

◆ What Do You Think?

1. What are some ways to eat healthy?
2. What are some ways to help the environment?

◆ Background Knowledge ◆

LOHAS stands for "Lifestyles of Health and Sustainability." It refers to a group of people who are concerned about their health and the environment. They buy locally grown or organic food and fair trade products. They also try to help the environment by recycling and saving energy.

◆ Power Vocabulary ◆

• organic	growing or producing food without using artificial chemicals
• describe	to give an explanation of something
• consumer	a person who buys things
• sustainability	the ability to survive for a long time
• direct	having nothing else coming in between
• well-being	a healthy state of happiness and wealth
• mission	the goal of a person or group
• offer	to give something that someone needs or deserves
• distance	the space between two objects or places
• pesticide	a chemical that kills bugs

Living Responsibly

T07

Do you try to buy organic food, or products without a lot of plastic packaging? Do you care about not only your health but also the environment? If so, then you are part of the LOHAS movement.

LOHAS is a term that describes a certain type of consumer or company. It stands for "Lifestyles of Health and Sustainability." LOHAS members believe there is a direct link between the well-being of the environment and the well-being of people. So, the mission of the movement is to encourage consumers and companies to care about both their personal well-being and the well-being of the environment.

One of the main ideas of the LOHAS movement is sustainability. It is not sustainable for human beings to continue to use so much oil and other natural resources. If we do, there will be nothing left in the future for our children. So, LOHAS members support companies that offer goods and services that use fewer of these essential resources.

For example, LOHAS members focus on buying both local food and organic food. Local food does not have to be shipped long distances, which means that less fuel is used when transporting it. And organic food is grown without pesticides. This is important because it helps keep our water supply free from harmful chemicals.

The LOHAS group is growing rapidly, as more people learn about the benefits of this kind of lifestyle. LOHAS members want more and more consumers and companies to join their movement. They hope that someday everyone will care about health and the environment.

1st Reading _____ **min** _____ **sec** **2nd Reading** _____ **min** _____ **sec** (259 words)

Guessing word meaning ··· Sometimes the meaning of a word is explained in the previous or following sentence.

► What does the word 'support' mean in line **13**?

Reading Comprehension

Choose the best answers.

1. What is the passage mainly about?

a. global warming
b. environmental organizations
c. the benefits of organic food
d. the mission of LOHAS movement

2. According to the passage, why do LOHAS members buy local food?

a. because it is not grown with pesticides
b. because it does not use plastic packaging
c. because it uses less fuel when being transported
d. because it keeps our water supply safe from harmful chemicals

3. What are the best words for (A) and (B)?

> LOHAS members believe there is a link between ____(A)____ well-being and ____(B)____ well-being.

a. animals' – plants'
b. the environment's – people's
c. animals' – people's
d. the environment's – animals'

4. You are NOT part of the LOHAS movement if you ______________.

a. buy local food
b. buy organic food
c. care about the environment
d. buy products with a lot of plastic packaging

5. What is NOT used when growing organic food?

a. oil　b. plastic　c. animals　d. pesticides

Write the answers in full sentences.

1. What is the mission of the LOHAS movement?

____

2. What companies do LOHAS members support?

____

3. What will happen if people continue to use too much of natural resources?

____

Graphic Organizer

◆ **Fill in the blanks to explain the mission and practice of the LOHAS movement.**

LOHAS Movement

Mission: to __________ consumers and companies to care about their well-being and well-being of the __________

Practice:
1. to support companies that use fewer __________ resources
2. to buy __________ food to use less fuel
3. to buy __________ food that does not use harmful pesticides

Vocabulary Build-up

◆ **Choose the best words to fill in the blanks.**

1. The company trys to attract more __________ with its new advertisement.
a. farmers b. officials c. criminals d. consumers

2. The __________ of the UN is to spread peace and protect our world.
a. mission b. distance c. resource d. well-being

3. Fruits grown using __________ farming techniques are popular these days.
a. plastic b. organic c. packaged d. essential

◆ **Choose the words with similar meanings to the underlined words.**

1. Words cannot <u>describe</u> the beauty of this scene.
a. decide b. expect c. explain d. response

2. Harry <u>offered</u> everyone a piece of pie and a glass of wine.
a. bought b. provided c. consumed d. transported

Word Power

The suffix -ic is used to make adjectives and show the quality or the relation to something.
- *Organic* food tastes a lot better.
- I'm trying to find *scientific* evidence to prove my point.

The Secret Garden

Unit 08

• **Theme** > Literature • **Reading Strategy** > Identifying an author's purpose

What Do You Think?

1. Who is your favorite author and why?
2. What kinds of stories do you like to read?

Background Knowledge

Frances Hodgson Burnett wrote famous children's stories such as *Little Lord Fauntleroy* and *The Secret Garden*. She was born in 1849 in England, but for most of her life she lived in the United States. When she was growing up she loved making up stories, and most of them took place in England. She published her first story when she was only eighteen.

Power Vocabulary

• orphan	a child who has lost both parents
• bear	to put up with
• maid	a female that does household chores as a job
• spot	a place
• nurse	to look after carefully
• barely	hardly; only just
• return	to come back
• positive	moving in a good direction
• rude	rough in manners or behavior; not gentle
• complain	to express displeasure or unhappiness

A Door to Happiness

T08

Book Review

Although *The Secret Garden* was written in 1911, it remains a children's favorite because of its fascinating story, colorful characters and positive message.

The Secret Garden is the story of an orphan named Mary. She lives with her uncle, Mr. Craven, in the English countryside. Mr. Craven rarely stays at home, though. His wife died and he can't bear to be in the house she used to live in.

Mary is lonely and unhappy, but luckily a maid named Martha spends time with her. Martha tells Mary about a hidden garden that used to be Mrs. Craven's favorite spot. Mary finds the garden, but most of the flowers have died. Mary decides to make it her special project, and she slowly nurses it back to life. As the garden grows, Mary becomes happier.

Then, Mary becomes friends with Colin, Mr. Craven's son. Colin is sick and he almost never leaves his room. Colin can barely walk, but Mary helps him walk to the garden. When Mr. Craven returns to the house, he is delighted to see that his son can walk and that the children have become friends, thanks to the secret garden.

The story is fun to read, and it also has an important message for young readers about positive change. Both Mary and Colin are rude and unpleasant at first. They complain a lot and only think about themselves. Through hard work and a relationship with nature, they learn to care about others and to think positively. Just like the garden, with a little love and care they are able to grow into something beautiful.

1st Reading _____ min _____ sec 2nd Reading _____ min _____ sec (267 words)

Identifying an author's purpose ··· Authors share their attitudes on different subjects to explain, describe, entertain or persuade with their text.

► What is the purpose of this article?

Reading Comprehension

◆ Choose the best answers.

1. What is the passage mainly about?

a. how to take care of a garden
b. an orphan who never gave up
c. lessons from *The Secret Garden*
d. a boy who showed positive change

2. Which is NOT true about *The Secret Garden*?

a. Colin is an orphan.
b. Mr. Craven is Mary's uncle.
c. Mary used to be lonely and unhappy.
d. The secret garden was Mrs. Craven's favorite spot.

3. What is Mary's special project in the story?

a. taking care of Colin
b. making friends with her maid
c. nursing the garden back to life
d. uncovering of Mrs. Craven's secret

4. How did Mary and Colin change in the story?

a. rude → caring b. kind → rude
c. unpleasant → negative d. pleasant → unpleasant

5. *The Secret Garden* has an important message for readers about ______________.

a. secrets b. gardening
c. a family d. positive change

◆ Write the answers in full sentences.

1. Why is Mr. Craven rarely at home?

____

2. Who tells Mary about the hidden garden?

____

3. Why did Colin almost always stay in his room?

____

Graphic Organizer

◆ **Fill in the blanks to explain *The Secret Garden*.**

The Secret Garden	
Characters	• Mary, Mr. Craven, Colin Martha
Story Line	• Mary finds the __________ garden and takes care of it. • Mary becomes __________ with Colin. • Mary helps Colin __________ to the garden.
Message	• Hard work and a relationship with __________ can teach people to __________ about others and think __________.

Vocabulary Build-up

◆ **Choose the best words to fill in the blanks.**

1. The ______________ was happy to meet her new parents.

a. maid b. orphan c. nurse d. doctor

2. I have never heard you ______________ about your boss.

a. hide b. discover c. provide d. complain

3. You need to be ______________ to overcome this situation.

a. positive b. negative c. possible d. unpleasant

◆ **Choose the words with similar meanings to the underlined words.**

1. Nancy's piano is dusty because she <u>barely</u> plays it.

a. never b. rarely c. always d. sometimes

2. I remember the exact <u>spot</u> where the accident happened.

a. car b. school c. place d. street

Word Power

The suffix –ive is used in adjectives to add the meaning of 'belonging to' or 'the quality of.'

- It is important to have a *positive* attitude.
- My teeth are so *sensitive* that I can't eat anything cold.

Bacteria Vs. Viruses

Unit 09

• **Theme** > Health • **Reading Strategy** > Comparing and contrasting

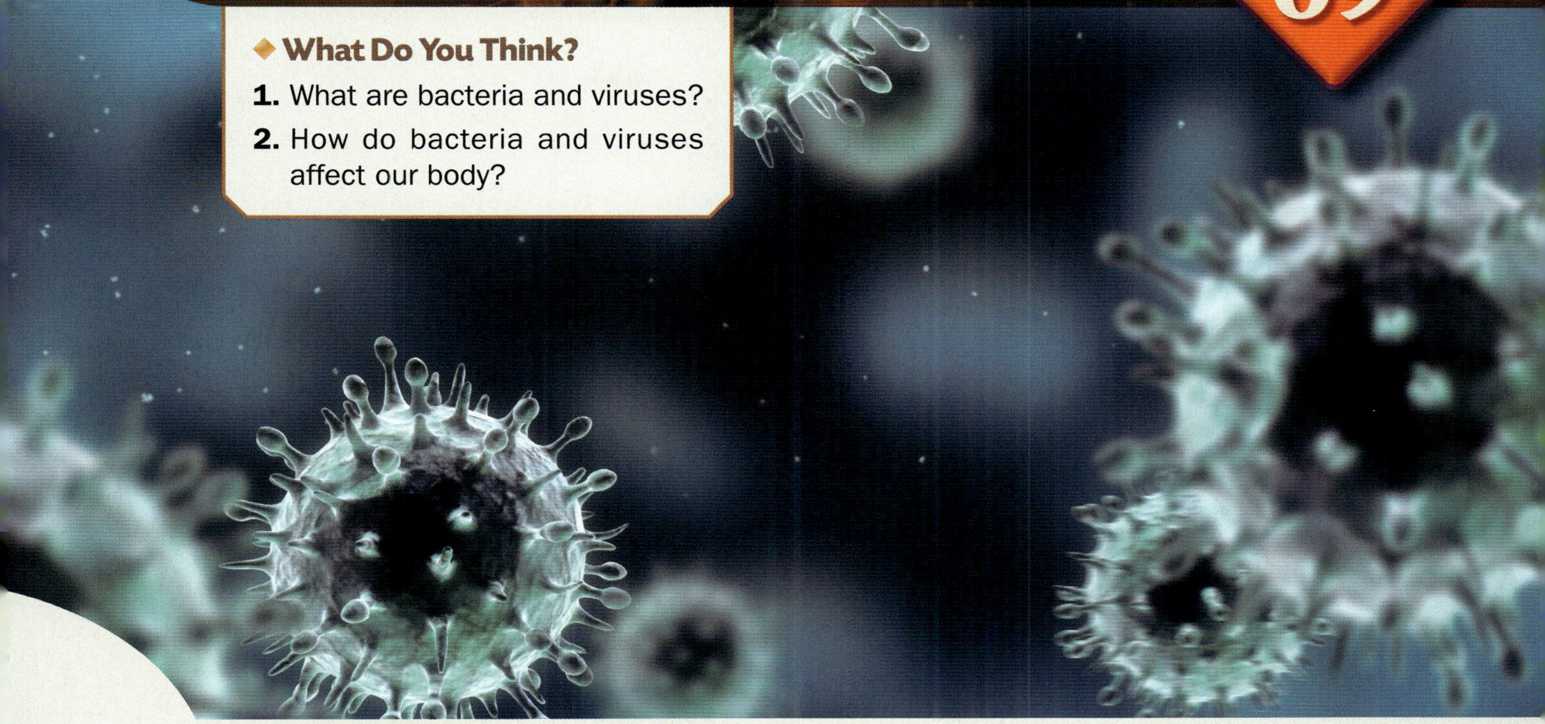

What Do You Think?

1. What are bacteria and viruses?
2. How do bacteria and viruses affect our body?

Background Knowledge

It is thought that both bacteria and viruses have existed since the beginning of time. Bacteria are considered the earliest known life forms. Sometimes, they can lead to minor infections, but in most cases, they do positive things. On the other hand, viruses don't have any good effects on people. They can even lead to serious diseases.

Power Vocabulary

negative	expressing disagreement; harmful or bad
outweigh	to be more important in value
infection	the process of making someone get a disease
valuable	worth a lot of money
medication	a drug to treat or cure illness
patience	the ability to remain calm or do something for a long time
disappear	to no longer happen or exist
spread	to cover a large area or to gradually affect
exchange	to give and receive at the same time
contact	the act of touching or meeting someone

Good Vs. Evil

T09

What do you think of when you hear the words bacteria and viruses? Many people think negative things. We're usually told to stay away from places with bacteria and people with viruses in order to stay clean and healthy.

But did you know that just 1% of bacteria types are harmful? Actually, it is almost impossible to live without bacteria. Almost 50% of oxygen is made by bacteria and they even exist in our body. Fortunately, their benefits outweigh their bad effects. They help prevent infections and create valuable vitamins such as vitamin K. Also, nutritious foods like yogurt and cheese cannot be made without bacteria.

Viruses are found wherever there is life and have probably existed since living cells first evolved. Because viruses are always changing, medication seldom works against them. When they make us ill, the best cure is simply patience. After some time, they usually disappear. Some forms of cancer, the common cold, and other diseases are all produced by viruses. They do nothing to help our lives and can even lead to death.

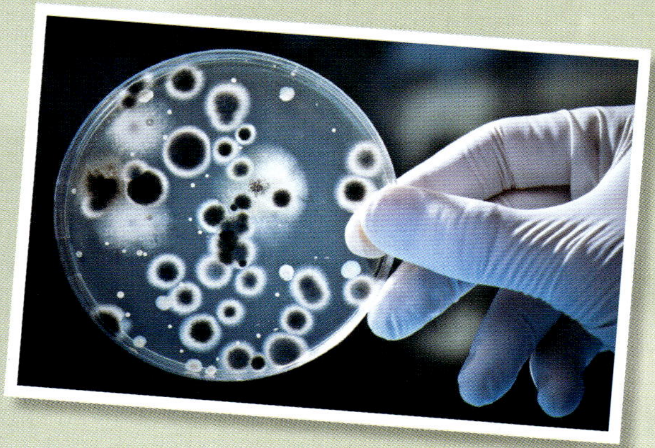

Though there are many differences between bacteria and viruses, the way they spread is similar. We can be infected through coughing, sneezing, touching another person, and exchanging bodily fluids. To remain healthy, we should avoid contact with sick people. If we do interact with them, we should wash our hands frequently. To avoid more serious infections, we should eat healthy food and get plenty of rest. Then our bodies can become stronger and fight off bacteria and viruses successfully.

1st Reading _____ min _____ sec 2nd Reading _____ min _____ sec (256 words)

Comparing and contrasting ··· Comparing and contrasting is used to show how certain things or ideas are similar or different from one another.

► What are the similarities of bacteria and viruses?

Reading Comprehension

Choose the best answers.

1. What is the passage mainly about?

a. what is inside our body
b. how to prevent illnesses
c. features of the common cold
d. the effects of bacteria and viruses

2. What percentage of bacteria types are harmful?

a. 1% b. 10% c. 30% d. 50%

3. What are the best words for (A) and (B)?

The ____(A)____ of bacteria outweigh their ____(B)____ effects.

a. benefits – bad b. disadvantages – bad
c. benefits – good d. disadvantages – good

4. Which is NOT mentioned in the passage about viruses?

a. They can cause cancer.
b. They prevent infections.
c. They produce the common cold.
d. They often cannot be cured by medication.

5. To remain healthy, we should ____________.

a. take a lot of medication b. interact with strangers
c. go to the hospital regularly d. avoid contact with sick people

Write the answers in full sentences.

1. What nutritious foods are created by bacteria?

____

2. How are bacteria and viruses different?

____

3. What should we do to avoid serious infections?

____

Graphic Organizer

◆ **Fill in the blanks to compare bacteria with viruses.**

	Bacteria	Viruses
Similarities	• They are spread through ________, ________, touching another person, and ________ bodily fluids.	
Differences	• Just 1% of them are ________. • Their ________ outweigh their bad effects. • They help prevent ________ and create valuable ________.	• ________ seldom works against them. • They produce ________, the common cold, and other diseases. • They can lead to ________.

Vocabulary Build-up

◆ **Choose the best words to fill in the blanks.**

1. You have to have ________ and wait until the results are released.
a. minds b. effects c. contact d. patience

2. I try to find people's positive aspects rather than their ________ ones.
a. negative b. common c. healthy d. generous

3. We built a factory in this town because the benefits ________ the problems.
a. lack b. equal c. outweigh d. support

◆ **Choose the words with opposite meanings to the underlined words.**

1. Helping others was a <u>valuable</u> experience for me.
a. serious b. strange c. useless d. important

2. The woman <u>disappeared</u> without a word and never came back.
a. spread b. showed c. returned d. finished

Word Power

The suffix –ence or –ance is used with nouns to add the meaning of 'state' or 'process.'
- I have two tickets left for tonight's *performance*.
- Andrew doesn't have the *patience* to complete the task.

Mardi Gras

Unit 10

• Theme > Festivals • Reading Strategy > Scanning

◆ **What Do You Think?**

1. What is the most memorable festival you have been to?
2. Have you ever celebrated Mardi Gras?

◆ Background Knowledge ◆

Mardi Gras is mostly celebrated in New Orleans, U.S.A. It was the ancient Romans who brought the idea of celebrating before Lent, which is a religious holiday for Catholics. During Lent, Catholic people try to make themselves pure by giving up something they enjoy. So before Lent, everyone eats a lot and has fun for two weeks!

◆ Power Vocabulary ◆

• holiday	a day on which work is not done by law or custom
• capital	a place that a certain activity or object is centered around
• celebration	a special, enjoyable event
• last	to continue existing or happening for a particular time
• incredible	beyond belief or understanding
• stuff	to fill tightly with a material
• invite	to offer a request to join an event or activity
• attraction	somewhere or something that provides pleasure
• organize	to prepare or arrange an activity or event
• experience	to go through

Magical Mardi Gras!

Advertisement

Mardi Gras was originally a Catholic holiday, but these days anyone can enjoy this exciting festival. Mardi Gras is French for "Fat Tuesday." For Catholics, the idea behind Mardi Gras was to eat and party before Lent, a Catholic holiday that begins each year on a Wednesday. During Lent, you must give up enjoyable things, such as eating certain foods. The French brought this festival to the United States when they came to Louisiana in 1699. Now, New Orleans is the Mardi Gras capital of the world.

Mardi Gras celebrations last for two weeks, so you have a great deal of time to enjoy yourself. You can see enormous parades, hear incredible jazz music, and eat until you are stuffed … and then eat some more! One thing you might eat during Mardi Gras is "king cake." Each cake has a small plastic baby inside. If you find the baby in your piece of cake, you get to be king or queen of the party! If you're lucky, you might even be invited to a ball where everyone wears costumes and beautiful masks.

Be sure not to miss the main attraction: the parades! There is one every day for two weeks, and each one is organized by a group or "krewe." The members of the krewe ride the floats and throw things to the audience, like beads and wooden coins called dubloons.

Many people say Mardi Gras is one of the best festivals in the world. But don't take our word for it — come to New Orleans and experience this unique holiday for yourself!

1st Reading ____ min ____ sec 2nd Reading ____ min ____ sec (264 words)

Scanning ··· Scanning is looking quickly at something without reading it carefully, often looking for some particular information such as key words or ideas.

▶ Who brought Mardi Gras to the United States?

Reading Comprehension

Choose the best answers.

1. What is the passage mainly about?

a. how to make king cake
b. the features of New Orleans
c. the different kinds of Catholic holidays
d. the origin and attractions of Mardi Gras

2. Mardi Gras was originally a(n) ______________ holiday.

a. national　　b. American
c. Catholic　　d. worldwide

3. What happens when you find a plastic baby in your piece of king cake?

a. You get some money for a prize.
b. You become the leader of a krewe.
c. You get a golden trophy for a prize.
d. You become king or queen of the party.

4. How long do Mardi Gras celebrations last?

a. for two days　　b. for two weeks
c. for two months　　d. for two years

5. Which is NOT true about Mardi Gras parades?

a. They are organized by krewes.
b. Krewes invite you to eat king cake.
c. They are held every day for two weeks.
d. Members of krewes throw things to the audience.

Write the answers in full sentences.

1. What was the original idea behind Mardi Gras for Catholics?

____

2. Where is the Mardi Gras capital of the world?

____

3. What activity would you like to do the most at a Mardi Gras celebration?

____

Graphic Organizer

◆ **Fill in the blanks to give information about Mardi Gras.**

Mardi Gras

When	• for ________ weeks before Lent
Where	• New Orleans
Key Events	• eating king cake: People who find a plastic ________ become king or queen of the party. • parades: ________ members organize the parades, ride the floats and throw things to the audience.

Vocabulary Build-up

◆ **Choose the best words to fill in the blanks.**

1. South Korea is the kimchi ____________ of the world.

a. city b. capital c. celebration d. experience

2. I didn't go to the party because I wasn't ____________.

a. thrown b. invited c. captured d. demanded

3. How many days does the festival ____________ for?

a. last b. wear c. throw d. become

◆ **Choose the words with similar meanings to the underlined words.**

1. Angela organized a surprised party for her sister.

a. wore b. found c. enjoyed d. arranged

2. The concert was so incredible that everyone wanted an encore.

a. stuffed b. horrible c. amazing d. enormous

Word Power

The suffix –able or –ible is used in adjectives and means 'capable of.'

- I feel *responsible* for your failure.
- The research will have an *incredible* impact on the existing theory.

Maps

Unit 11

• **Theme** > History • **Reading Strategy** > Finding main ideas

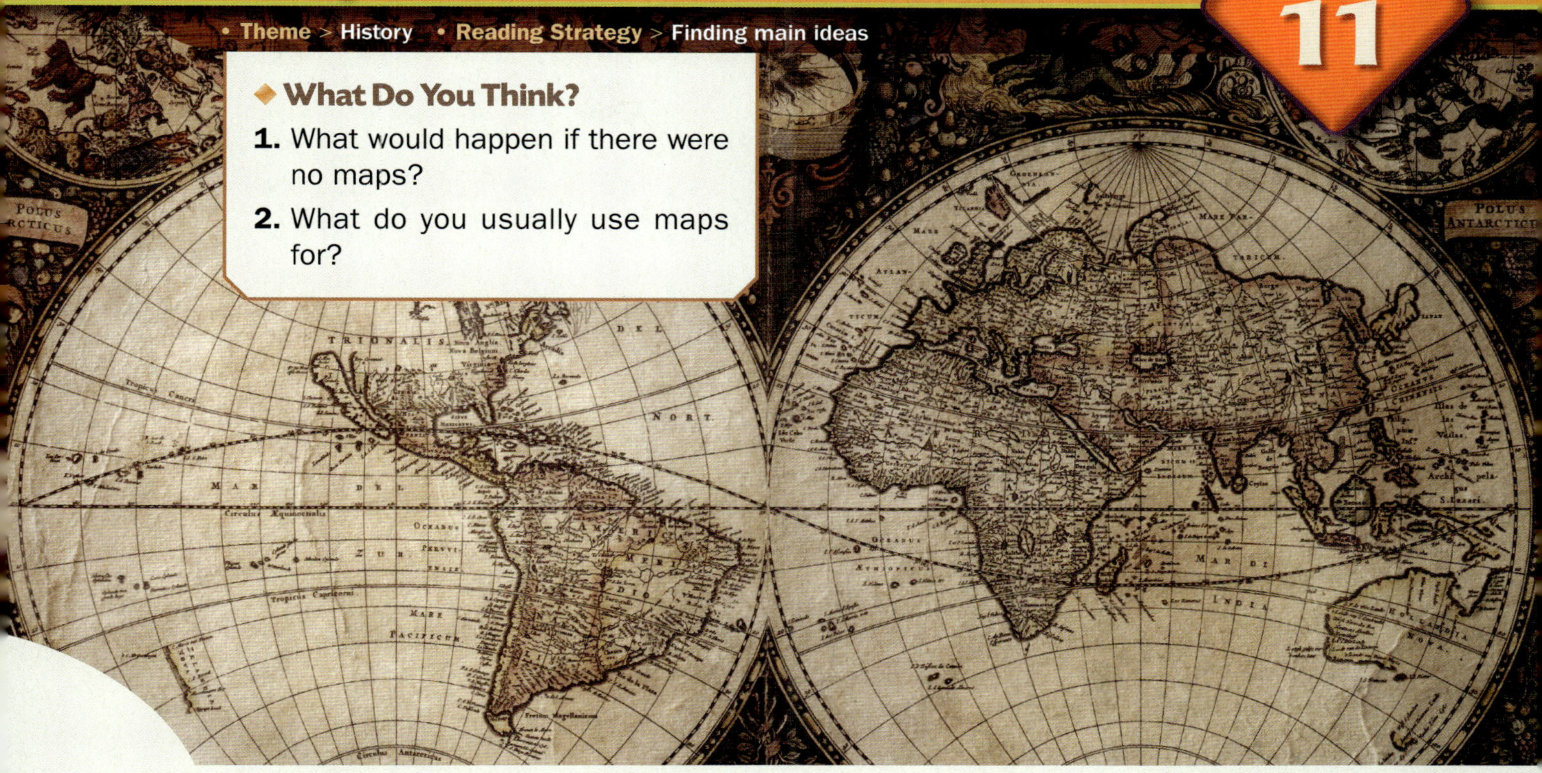

◆ What Do You Think?

1. What would happen if there were no maps?
2. What do you usually use maps for?

◆ Background Knowledge ◆

A map is a picture or a model of a space that explains where each object is in relation to other objects. It shows what a place looks like, or how to get from one place to another. The oldest maps that still exist today were carved into stone tablets. They were found in the ruins of ancient Babylon and are over 4,000 years old.

◆ Power Vocabulary ◆

- wonder — to be curious about
- explore — to travel to a place in order to learn about it
- entire — having all the parts; whole
- carve — to make an object by cutting it from stone or wood
- revolution — a sudden or major change in action and thought
- transport — to carry something or someone from one place to another
- complex — having many details that make it difficult to understand
- satellite — an object that is sent into space to travel around the Earth
- advance — to improve; to move forward
- convenient — easy to use

Picturing the World T11

Do you wonder what Times Square in New York looks like? All you have to do is to go online. You can easily find a street map for New York, including pictures of every street.

Of course, this was not always possible. A long time ago, people didn't know what the rest of the world looked like. They used maps to check trade routes and to explore the world piece by piece. As people traveled further, they were able to update the maps and slowly create a picture of the entire Earth.

The first map that showed the whole world was made in 1507. At first, maps were carved in stone. Stone is heavy to carry, however, so people began to carve maps into wood and metal. When the printing press was invented in the 15th century, it was a revolution for mapmakers. They were able to print their maps on paper, which is easier to produce and transport.

Today, we often use complex technology to make maps. There are satellite maps that show us what places look like from the sky, and navigation maps that show us exactly where we are at any time. You can even use maps online to find a store or restaurant near you.

In a fairly short time, we have gone from stone tablets to complex digital maps. As technology advances, the way we use maps is changing. But one thing hasn't changed: we continue to develop more detailed and convenient maps in order to explore our world.

1st Reading _____ min _____ sec 2nd Reading _____ min _____ sec (254 words)

Finding main ideas ··· The main idea of a paragraph tells the topic of the paragraph. The topic tells what most of the sentences are about.

► What is the main idea of the third paragraph?

Reading Comprehension

Choose the best answers.

1. What is the passage mainly about?

a. the roles of satellites
b. the future of navigation maps
c. the development of maps
d. the history of the printing press

2. Satellite maps show us what places look like from the ______________.

a. sky
b. car
c. ground
d. computer

3. What do navigation maps do?

a. They let us print maps on paper.
b. They let us go online to find a store.
c. They show exactly where we are at any time.
d. They show how places look like from the sky.

4. What are the best words for (A) and (B)?

We have advanced from ______(A)______ to complex ______(B)______.

a. stone tablets – paper maps
b. wood maps – digital maps
c. stone tablets – digital maps
d. paper maps – navigation maps

5. Which is NOT true according to the passage?

a. Maps were carved into wood and metal at first.
b. Paper maps were easier to produce and transport.
c. The printing press was a revolution for mapmakers.
d. The first map that showed the whole world was made in 1507.

Write the answers in full sentences.

1. What did people use maps for a long time ago?

____

2. Why was the invention of the printing press a revolution for mapmakers?

____

3. Why do we continue to develop more detailed and convenient maps?

____

Graphic Organizer

◆ **Fill in the blanks to explain the development of maps.**

Development of Maps

Past	Present
• Maps were used for checking ________ routes and exploring the world. • The first map of the whole world was made in ________. • Materials have changed from ________ to ________ and metal, then to paper.	• ________ maps: show us the world from the sky • ________ maps: tell us exactly where we are • ________ maps: are useful to find a store or restaurant near us

Vocabulary Build-up

◆ **Choose the best words to fill in the blanks.**

1. Ben ____________ his name into the tree with his knife.

a. ripped b. carved c. painted d. updated

2. The company decided to ____________ the goods by ship, not by plane.

a. report b. produce c. develop d. transport

3. Emily wants to travel to different countries and ____________ the world.

a. hate b. reject c. explore d. include

◆ **Choose the words with opposite meanings to the underlined words.**

1. This is a <u>convenient</u> place for me to take a rest.

a. cozy b. close c. uneasy d. comfortable

2. The teacher had a tough time explaining the <u>complex</u> history of Asia.

a. simple b. advanced c. outdated d. complicated

Word Power

The prefix trans– is used to add the meaning of 'across,' 'beyond,' or 'on the opposite side.'

- Mosquito bites can *transmit* malaria.
- The train *transports* millions of workers every day.

Rosa Parks

Unit 12

• Theme > People • Reading Strategy > Understanding sequences

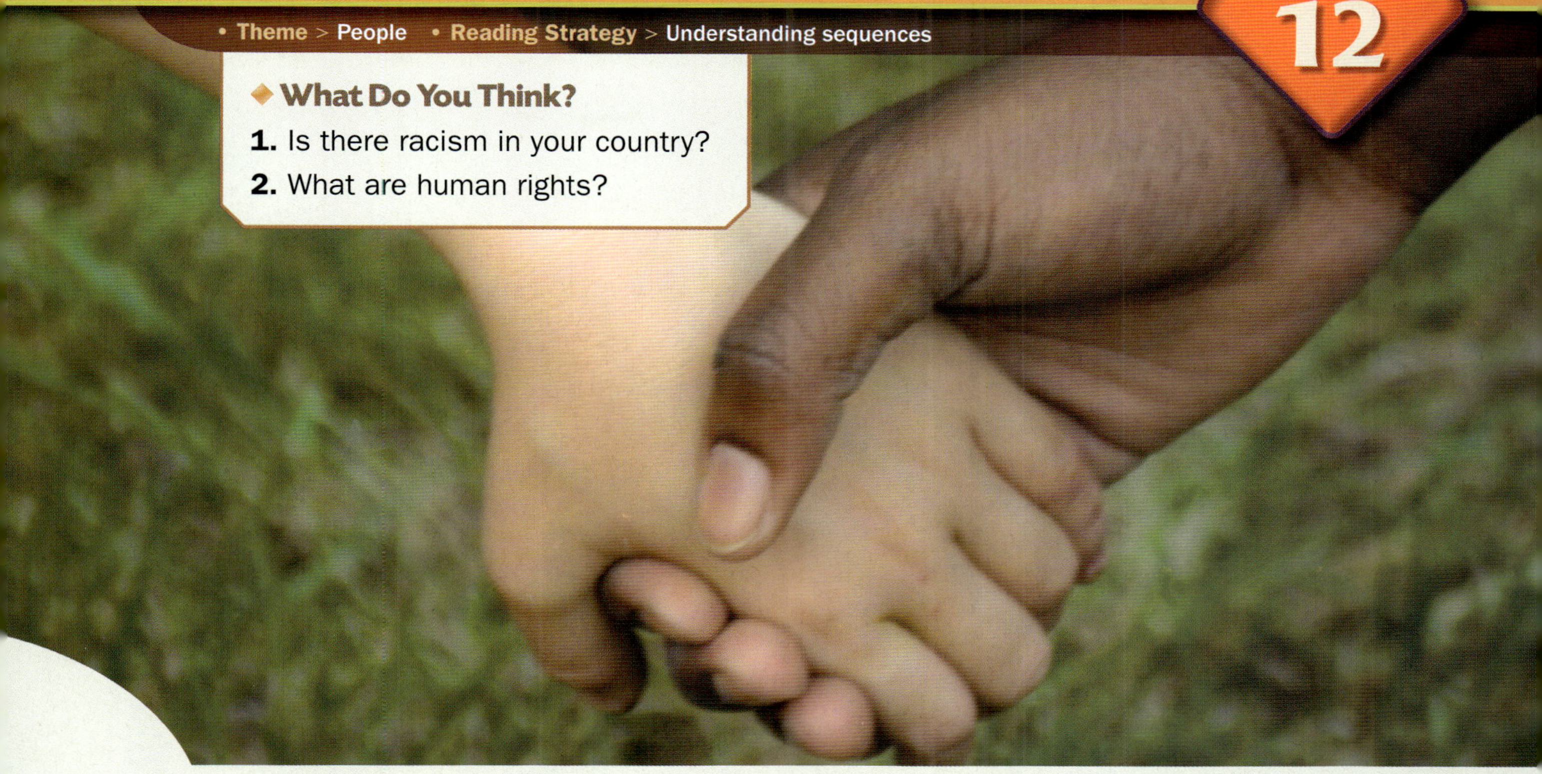

What Do You Think?

1. Is there racism in your country?
2. What are human rights?

Background Knowledge

By the 20th century, the U.S. government demanded laws to give equal treatment to black people. Many white people became upset by this. As violence grew, the black community began to fight against the inequality in society. Between 1950 and 1980, leaders like Martin Luther King, Jr. participated in the Civil Rights Movement. It helped create the social equality we enjoy today.

Power Vocabulary

- divide — to separate into different pieces
- inequality — not being treated equally
- secretary — a person who handles work for a boss or an organization
- abandon — to give up
- arrest — to put into jail for doing something illegal
- bold — fearless
- spark — to create; to produce
- unfair — not having the same opportunities and advantages
- treatment — action or behavior toward a person, animal, etc.
- regard — to look upon or think of

The Struggle for Equality

T12

Biography

An iconic figure of the Civil Rights Movement, Rosa Parks was called "the first lady of civil rights." She was born on February 4, 1913. When she was young, she watched her white classmates ride on a different section of the bus. Under the "Jim Crow" laws, blacks and whites were divided into different sections on buses and in other public areas.

During this time, only 7% of the black population had a high school diploma. In spite of this, Rosa finished her high school education. After her studies, she became actively involved in the fight against inequality in society. She became a volunteer secretary for the National Association for the Advancement of Colored People (NAACP).

Rosa's role in the Civil Rights Movement became even more significant when she boarded a bus in 1955. She sat in the black section but as the bus moved along, the seats became full. The driver told Rosa to abandon her seat for the white people standing up. She refused. The driver called the police and she was arrested. Her arrest caused many personal problems for her and her family. There was a lot of racism against black people at that time, so many people were angry at her.

This single bold act by Rosa Parks sparked the beginning of the Civil Rights Movement in the United States. Her courage showed society the unfair treatment of blacks. She is regarded as a symbol of the Civil Rights Movement and as a fighter against racial inequality. From her strength, we can learn to always stand up — or sit down — for our beliefs.

1st Reading _____ min _____ sec 2nd Reading _____ min _____ sec (266 words)

Understanding sequences ··· Stories are often told in the order in which the events occurred — from beginning to ending.

▶ What did Rosa Parks do after finishing her high school education?

Reading Comprehension

Choose the best answers.

1. What is the passage mainly about?

   a. bus-related laws
   b. the formation of the Jim Crow laws
   c. Rosa Parks' family
   d. Rosa Parks and the Civil Rights Movement

2. What said that blacks and whites must be separated in public areas?

   a. the Jim Crow laws
   b. the NAACP laws
   c. the Rosa Parks laws
   d. the Civil Rights act

3. What happened when Rosa Parks refused to abandon her seat for the white people?

   a. She was arrested by the police.
   b. The Civil Rights Movement failed.
   c. She was abandoned by the NAACP.
   d. The driver allowed her to stay on the bus.

4. Rosa Parks is regarded as ______________.

   a. a fighter against black people
   b. a leader for volunteer secretarys
   c. the first lady among black people
   d. a symbol of the Civil Rights Movement

5. Which is NOT true about Rosa Parks?

   a. She did not finish high school.
   b. She fought against inequality in society.
   c. She was called "the first lady of civil rights."
   d. She was a volunteer secretary for the NAACP.

Write the answers in full sentences.

1. What happened to Rosa Parks after her arrest?

   ____

2. What was the effect of Rosa Parks' bold act?

   ____

3. What can we learn from Rosa Parks' strength?

   ____

Graphic Organizer

◆ **Fill in the blanks to explain Rosa Parks' life.**

Rosa Parks

Her Childhood
- She was born on February 4, 1913.
- Blacks and whites were __________ in public areas under the __________ __________ laws.

Her Adulthood
- She became a volunteer secretary for the __________.
- She didn't give up her __________ on a bus and was __________.
- She sparked the __________ __________ movement.
- She was regarded as a fighter against racial __________.

Vocabulary Build-up

◆ **Choose the best words to fill in the blanks.**

1. My mother __________ the chocolate bar into two parts.
a. arrested b. divided c. involved d. abandoned

2. The workers complained about their __________ salary.
a. equal b. active c. unfair d. rewarding

3. Patrick was __________ enough to fight against his enemies.
a. bold b. normal c. iconic d. personal

◆ **Choose the words with similar meanings to the underlined words.**

1. John and Jane's love sparked a great romantic movie idea.
a. told b. ended c. caused d. stopped

2. I regard a person's character before deciding to become friends with them.
a. prove b. create c. wonder d. consider

Word Power

The prefix un– is used to add the meaning of 'not,' 'against,' or 'opposite.'
- It is *unfair* that I have to pay more.
- Don't waste time doing *unnecessary* things.

Reptiles

Unit 13

• Theme > Animals • Reading Strategy > Recalling facts and details

◆ **What Do You Think?**

1. What is your favorite reptile?
2. Do you think reptiles can be good pets?

◆ Background Knowledge ◆

Scientists organize all living things into categories, and each one has a Latin name. The animal group is called *Kingdom Animalia*, or the animal kingdom. Within this kingdom there are smaller groups called "classes." There are many different classes, and they are organized by how the animals reproduce or what they look like. Some of the main classes are mammals, birds, fish, and reptiles.

◆ Power Vocabulary ◆

- furry — covered with a soft hair
- mammal — a warm-blooded animal that gives birth to its babies
- feature — an important part of something
- continent — a large body of land differing from an island
- species — a class of living things that have common characteristics
- waterproof — not allowing water to pass through; unaffected by water
- aquatic — having to do with water
- enemy — a group that is against someone or something
- reputation — the opinion that people have about how good or bad something is
- villain — an evil person or thing

Amazing Reptiles

T13

Are you afraid of reptiles? Do they seem unfriendly because they aren't furry like mammals? Don't turn away because of their scaly skin: They have some truly unique features. The reptile class includes more than 8,000 species, and they can be found in every continent except Antarctica. The most common reptiles are lizards, snakes, turtles, and crocodiles.

Although each reptile species is different, they have many things in common. For one thing, they all lay eggs on land. And amazingly, their babies are independent as soon as they break out of their shells. Also, all reptiles are cold-blooded and can't control their body temperature. That's why many reptiles lay in the sun to warm up. Most reptiles can't breathe underwater, even if they have waterproof skin. Even aquatic turtles must sometimes come up for air.

Among the different species of reptiles, chameleons and turtles are known to be particularly interesting. Chameleons respond to outside temperatures and change the color of their skin according to it. Sometimes this helps them to hide from enemies. On the other hand, turtles have a reputation for slowness. But, in fact, they are the fastest reptiles in the world: The Pacific leatherback turtle can swim up to 35 kilometers per hour. Also, they are the second largest reptiles, after the saltwater crocodile.

Although some reptiles like crocodiles can be quite dangerous, most are harmless. Even though they're usually the villains in movies and TV shows, many of them, such as snakes, iguanas, and turtles, make great pets. So next time you see a snake on the ground, don't run away — go and take a closer look!

1st Reading _____ min _____ sec 2nd Reading _____ min _____ sec (271 words)

Recalling facts and details ··· Facts and details explain more about the main statement with examples. They show the who, what, where, when, why, and how information about the main idea.

▶ What is amazing about the babies of reptiles?

Reading Comprehension

Choose the best answers.

1. What is the passage mainly about?

a. features of reptiles
b. the superiority of mammals
c. the classifications of animals
d. the different kinds of crocodiles

2. Which does NOT fit in the blank?

Reptiles can be found in ______________.

a. Asia b. Africa c. Antarctica d. South America

3. Which is NOT included in the reptile class?

a. fish b. lizards c. snakes d. turtles

4. Which is NOT a common feature of reptiles?

a. They lay eggs on land.
b. They can breathe underwater.
c. They are cold-blooded animals.
d. They are independent the moment they break out of their shell.

5. Why do reptiles lay in the sun?

a. because they can't breathe underwater
b. because they need to hide from enemies
c. because they need to change the color of their skin
d. because they need to control their body temperature

Write the answers in full sentences.

1. How do chameleons hide from enemies?

____

2. What is the fastest reptile in the world?

____

3. What is the largest reptile in the world?

____

Graphic Organizer

◆ **Fill in the blanks to explain characteristics of reptiles.**

Characteristics of Reptiles

Common Characteristics	Interesting Characteristics
• They lay __________ on land. • They are cold-blooded and can't __________ their body temperature. • They can't breathe __________.	• Chameleons change their skin __________ according to outside temperatures. • Turtles are the __________ reptiles in the world.

Vocabulary Build-up

◆ **Choose the best words to fill in the blanks.**

1. Asia is the largest ______________ in the world.

a. villains b. reptiles c. continent d. temperature

2. When it rains, I wear a(n) ______________ jacket so that I won't get wet.

a. furry b. dependent c. waterproof d. independent

3. I'm good at ______________ sports like water skiing and wakeboarding.

a. warm b. field c. track d. aquatic

◆ **Choose the words with similar meanings to the underlined words.**

1. John has an excellent <u>reputation</u> in the community.

a. name b. shell c. role d. change

2. Your facial <u>features</u> remind me of your parents.

a. enemies b. species c. mammals d. characteristics

Word Power

The suffix -proof is a combining form, meaning 'resistant' or 'protecting against.'
- Firefighters wear *fireproof* clothes.
- Umbrellas are made of *waterproof* material.

Science Fiction

Unit 14

• **Theme** > Technology • **Reading Strategy** > Finding main ideas

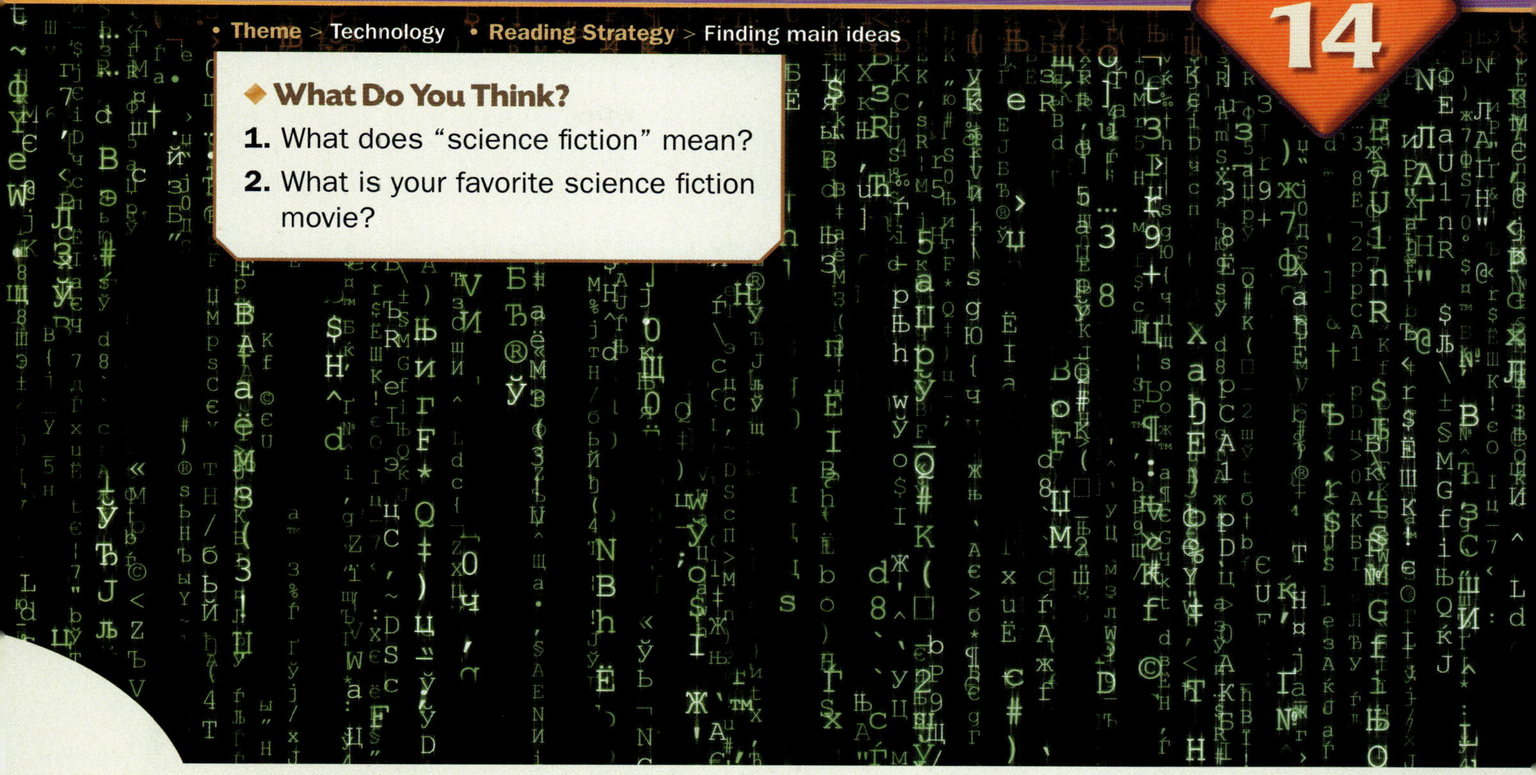

◆ What Do You Think?

1. What does "science fiction" mean?
2. What is your favorite science fiction movie?

◆ Background Knowledge ◆

There are many definitions of what science fiction or sci-fi is. It is similar to fantasy as it imagines a world that is not real. The difference is that in science fiction, science and technology play big roles. Most science fiction stories might eventually come true even if they're unlikely. They are often about technology that doesn't exist yet but might someday.

◆ Power Vocabulary ◆

• kidnap	to hold a person against their will
• reality	the state of being real
• distant	far apart in space or time
• stimulate	to cause to do
• force	to make someone do something that he/she doesn't want to do
• major	greater in size, extent, or importance
• fancy	not plain; decorative
• raise	to cause
• humanity	all the living people in the world
• universe	everything including the unexamined planets in outer space

A Whole New Universe

In the movie *The Matrix*, the main character, Neo, is kidnapped by a mysterious woman. He has two choices. One of them is to take a blue pill and return to the world he knows. The other choice is to take a red pill and learn the truth. Neo takes the red pill, and discovers that the world he knows is just images created by computers. The frightening reality is that humans are controlled by machines.

Part of the reason why *The Matrix* appeals to people is that, like most science fiction movies, it allows us to imagine a different world. Most of the elements of science fiction are things that could happen in the far distant future. Of course, people also enjoy science fiction because it features amazing machines or inventions. It's exciting to imagine what our lives would be like if we had those machines.

Perhaps the main reason that science fiction interests people is that it stimulates us to think about our world. The stories are about changes that our world is going through today. In many of the stories, however, the changes are negative: Humans have destroyed the Earth, as in the movie *Wall-E*, or have been taken over by computers, like in *The Matrix*. These movies force us to think about the dangerous effects of technology rather than the positive ones.

It's easy to see why science fiction is such a major genre. Watching these movies, you can imagine machines that don't exist yet. Even if you are not interested in fancy inventions, you are given a chance to think about our world. They raise basic questions about humanity's relationship to the universe.

1st Reading _____ min _____ sec 2nd Reading _____ min _____ sec (278 words)

Finding main ideas ··· The main idea of an article tells the topic of the article. The topic is what most of the sentences are about.

► What is the main idea of the passage?

Reading Comprehension

Choose the best answers.

1. What is the passage mainly about?

a. robots
b. technology
c. science fiction
d. outer space

2. Which is NOT mentioned as a reason why people like science fiction?

a. because it lets us imagine a different world
b. because it only focuses on unknown outer space
c. because it challenges us to think about our world
d. because the inventions and machines in it are amazing

3. Science fiction is about ______________ that our world is going through.

a. changes
b. dreams
c. reality
d. characters

4. What are the best words for (A) and (B)?

> Science fiction movies make us think about the ____(A)____ effects of technology rather than the ____(B)____ ones.

a. bad – negative
b. dangerous – positive
c. good – positive
d. realistic – imaginary

5. What does science fiction raise basic questions about?

a. aliens on other planets
b. humans' need for technology
c. robots that will take over the world
d. humanity's relationship to the universe

Write the answers in full sentences.

1. What are some examples of science fiction movies?

____

2. In *The Matrix*, what happened when Neo took the red pill?

____

3. What have humans done in the movie *Wall-E*?

____

Graphic Organizer

◆ **Fill in the blanks to explain the attractions of science fiction.**

Science Fiction's Attractions

- allow us to __________ a different world in the far distant future
- feature amazing __________ or __________
- stimulate us to think about our __________

↓

- raise basic questions about __________ relationship to the __________

Vocabulary Build-up

◆ **Choose the best words to fill in the blanks.**

1. Dan's father ______________ him to go to university and study law.

a. forced b. featured c. invented d. kidnapped

2. The company hopes to create the new product in the __________future.

a. main b. near c. quiet d. unique

3. The advertisements ______________ consumers to buy the digital camera.

a. imagined b. discovered c. interested d. stimulated

◆ **Choose the words with opposite meanings to the underlined words.**

1. What <u>major</u> problem must you deal with now?

a. great b. minor c. serious d. current

2. My Neighbor is better than my <u>distant</u> cousin.

a. main b. close c. quiet d. unique

Word Power

The suffix –ty occurs in nouns, meaning 'quality' or 'state.'

- All wars are against *humanity*.
- Shawn is worried about the *safety* of his children.

Animal Defenses

Unit 15

• **Theme** > Science • **Reading Strategy** > Classifying information

◆ **What Do You Think?**

1. How can animals survive in the wild?
2. How can animals be safe from their predators?

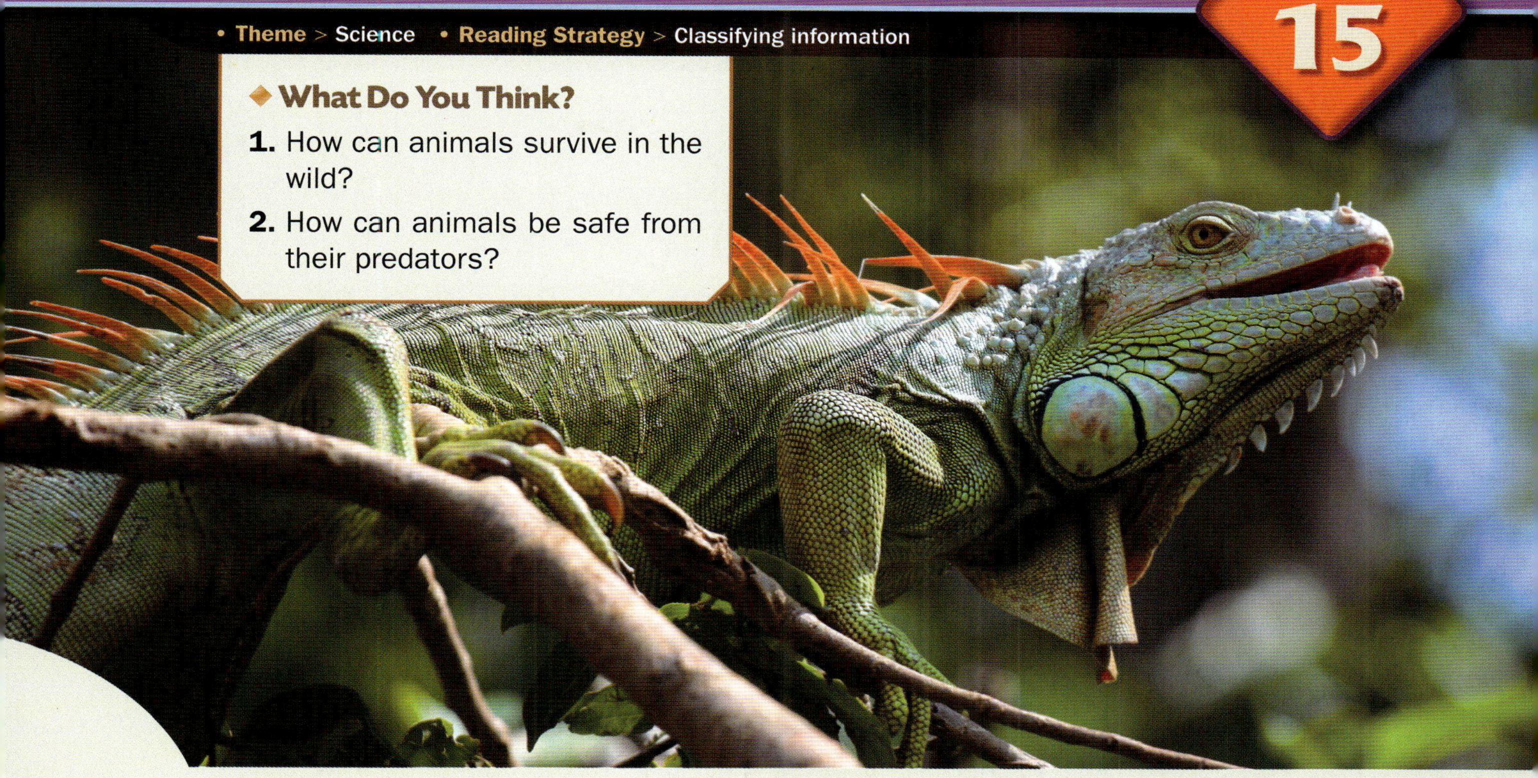

◆ Background Knowledge ◆

Animals depend on their physical features to help them get food, keep safe, and bear harsh weather. These physical features are called physical adaptations and help animals to survive. Physical adaptations develop over very long time. The shape of a bird's beak, the color of its feathers, and the shape of its wings are all examples of physical adaptations.

◆ Power Vocabulary ◆

• predator	an animal that kills and eats other animals
• defend	to protect something or someone
• individual	existing separately from other people or things
• pack	a large group
• scatter	to separate; to move in different directions
• direction	a line that someone or something moves on
• adapt	to fit into a certain environment
• involve	to include or contain as a necessary part
• evolve	to develop gradually
• spray	to cover a place or shower someone with drops of a liquid

Hide and Go Seek

T15

I f you were being chased by something, what would you do? You would probably hide, which is a basic way to escape predators. Many animals have unique ways to defend themselves if they can't escape.

The easiest way to be safe is to stay in a group. A predator is more likely to attack an animal that's alone. If a predator attacks the group, each individual is less likely to be caught because the predator will have to pick only one to chase after. Animals that travel in packs, like deer, usually scatter and run in different directions if they are being attacked. This confuses the predator.

Some animals are hard to see in the first place. Thanks to camouflage[1], they are able to blend in with their surroundings. For example, snow hares have white fur, making them hard to see in the snow where they live. There are even insects that live in trees and look exactly like twigs. These animals have adapted over thousands of years to look like their environment.

One of the most amazing types of defense involves chemicals. Some animals, like the monarch butterfly, have evolved to taste bad so that predators won't eat them. Others, like skunks, spray smelly chemicals at their predators to chase them away. If you've ever smelled a skunk, you know how effective that can be!

These methods of defense don't always work, but they have evolved over centuries to help each species survive. Without them, animals would be easily captured by predators and many species would die out.

1 camouflage: the way in which an animal's color or shape matches its surroundings

1st Reading _____ min _____ sec 2nd Reading _____ min _____ sec (259 words)

Classifying information ··· Classifying is to put things into groups according to their characteristics.

▶ Classify the types of animal defenses.

Reading Comprehension

Choose the best answers.

1. What is the passage mainly about?
   a. wildlife
   b. hunting animals
   c. predators
   d. animals' defenses

2. Which is NOT true according to the passage?
   a. Animals in packs can confuse their enemies.
   b. Deer run in the same direction when put in danger.
   c. A predator is more likely to attack an animal that's alone.
   d. Some animals have adapted to look like their environment.

3. The easiest way for animals to be safe is to stay ____________.
   a. in a group
   b. in the same area
   c. by themselves
   d. away from forests

4. How do skunks protect themselves from predators?
   a. by hiding
   b. by staying in a group
   c. by spraying smelly chemicals
   d. by blending in with their surroundings

5. Which animal uses camouflage to survive?
   a. a wolf
   b. a snow hare
   c. a skunk
   d. a monarch butterfly

Write the answers in full sentences.

1. How do deer act when being attacked?

   ____

2. What helps animals blend in with their surroundings?

   ____

3. How have monarch butterflies evolved?

   ____

Graphic Organizer

◆ **Fill in the blanks to explain how animals defend themselves.**

Ways Animals Defend Themselves

Making a Group	Camouflage	Using Chemicals
• travel in ________ • ________ when being attacked • example: ________	• blend in with their ________ • examples: snow hares, ________	• taste ________ • spray smelly ________ • examples: monarch butterflies, ________

Vocabulary Build-up

◆ **Choose the best words to fill in the blanks.**

1. Is it true that men ____________ from apes?

a. sprayed b. evolved c. blended d. resolved

2. Sharks are known as the ocean's top ____________.

a. twigs b. insects c. chemicals d. predators

3. Could you tell me which ____________ is the nearest station?

a. packs b. types c. species d. direction

◆ **Choose the words with similar meanings to the underlined words.**

1. Becoming a lawyer <u>involves</u> a lot of school work.

a. attacks b. adapts c. includes d. confuses

2. During her argument with her mother, Kate <u>defended</u> her opinion.

a. protected b. defeated c. captured d. rejected

Word Power

The suffix –or is used in nouns to indicate 'a person' or 'a thing.'

- Cats are the natural *predators* of birds.
- The *author* dedicated the book to his father.

The Galápagos Islands

Unit 16

• **Theme** > Places • **Reading Strategy** > Recognizing cause and effect

What Do You Think?

1. Have you ever heard of the Galápagos Islands?
2. What can we do to preserve the Galápagos Islands?

Background Knowledge

The Galápagos Islands are a group of thirteen islands that belong to Ecuador, a country in South America. More than 20,000 people live in the Galápagos, but most of the land is part of Ecuador's national park system. The islands are famous for their beautiful landscape and their unique plants and animals. They also have some of the most active volcanoes in the world.

Power Vocabulary

- wildlife — animals and plants that live in nature
- theory — an explanation or knowledge that has not yet been proven
- evolution — the way in which something gradually changes and develops
- native — belonging somewhere by birth
- attack — to cause harm; to act violently
- habitat — the natural environment of an animal or plant
- disturb — to stop the quietness or peace of a place or situation
- pollute — to make unclean with harmful chemicals or waste
- restriction — the state of being kept within limits
- remove — to get rid of

Incredible Islands

T16

If you were a scientist, you might want to research the Galápagos Islands. Even if not, you might wish to visit there. The Galápagos Islands are incredibly beautiful. And they are home to many rare plant and animal species. The wildlife in the Galápagos includes sea lions, giant turtles, and even a special kind of penguin. Charles Darwin was one of the first scientists to travel to the Galápagos, and his research there was central to his theory of evolution.

The islands were discovered by a Spanish priest in 1535, and since then pirates and colonists have brought in many non-native species, such as pigs, cows, and goats. These animals can be a big threat to the native species. They can attack the native species or destroy their habitats. Sadly, the native species are often not able to defend themselves. That is why there are now more foreign species than native species in the Galápagos.

There are also other dangers to the islands, like fishing, illegal hunting, and tourism. Tourism can be dangerous because big groups of people disturb the plants and animals, and cruise ships pollute the water.

So scientists and government workers have created restrictions for tourists and have gotten rid of some of the non-native species. The islands used to be on a list of endangered places, but in 2010 they were removed from the list thanks to the efforts of many people. Now, if you are lucky enough to visit the beautiful Galápagos Islands, you will be able to see unique plants and animals.

1st Reading ____ min ____ sec 2nd Reading ____ min ____ sec (258 words)

Recognizing cause and effect ··· When you read an article, ask how one thing causes the other.

► What put the Galápagos Islands in danger?

Reading Comprehension

Choose the best answers.

1. What is the passage mainly about?

a. the features of Ecuador
b. Charles Darwin's theories
c. introducing non-native species
d. the endangered Galápagos Islands

2. Who discovered the Galápagos in 1535?

a. a colonist
b. Charles Darwin
c. a Spanish priest
d. Christopher Columbus

3. Pirates and colonists have brought in many ______________ to the Galápagos.

a. giant turtles
b. cruise ships
c. native species
d. non-native species

4. What are the best words for (A) and (B)?

> Now there are more _____(A)_____ species than _____(B)_____ species in the Galápagos.

a. native – rare
b. foreign – native
c. native – foreign
d. foreign – common

5. Which is NOT mentioned as a danger to the Galápagos Islands?

a. fishing
b. coal mining
c. tourism
d. illegal hunting

Write the answers in full sentences.

1. How do the non-native species threaten the native species?

____

2. Why can tourism be dangerous to the Galápagos?

____

3. What steps were taken to protect the Galápagos Islands?

____

Graphic Organizer

◆ **Fill in the blanks to explain the threats to the Galápagos Islands and solutions.**

The Galápagos Islands

Threats	Solutions
• non-native species attacking the __________ species or destroying their __________ • people disturbing __________ and animals • cruise ships polluting the __________	• creating __________ for tourists • getting rid of some of the __________ species

Vocabulary Build-up

◆ **Choose the best words to fill in the blanks.**

1. The ______________ suggests that humans came from monkeys.

a. theory b. habitat c. danger d. restriction

2. ______________ occurs when animals adapt to new environments.

a. Wildlife b. Tourism c. Evolution d. Research

3. I've got an ink spot on my shirt and I can't ______________ it easily.

a. destroy b. remove c. praise d. pollute

◆ **Choose the words with similar meanings to the underlined words.**

1. Don't <u>disturb</u> my rest on the weekend.

a. keep b. protect c. display d. interrupt

2. The German army <u>attacked</u> Poland in 1939.

a. argued b. invaded c. defended d. discovered

Word Power

The prefix re– is used to add the meaning of 'again,' 'back,' or 'against.'
- Please *remove* all the viruses from my computer.
- I think *recycling* is necessary to reduce environmental pollution.

Check Your Reading Speed

Draw a bar on the table below indicating the speed of your 1st and 2nd reading of the main passages.

Reading Peak Book 3

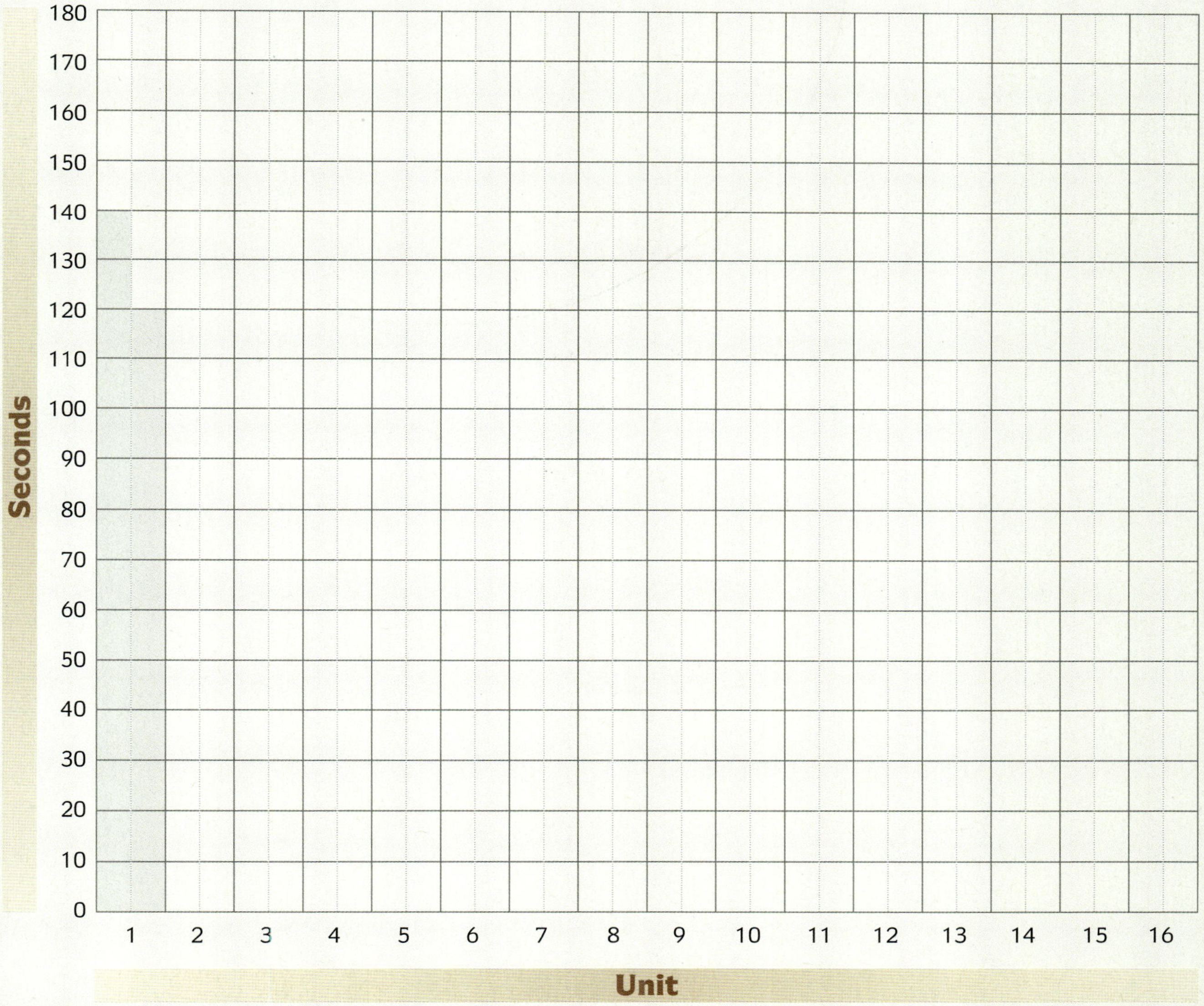

LEVEL GUIDE NE_Build & Grow Products

Category	Level	Kindergarten		Primary		
		Age 5-6	Age 7	Low Beginner	Beginner	High Beginner
Phonics	Phonics Show 1,2,3,4		■	■		
	Phonics Show Readers 1,2,3,4		■	■		
Reading	Reading Sketch Starter 1,2,3		■	■		
	Reading Sketch 1,2,3			■		
	Reading Sponge 1,2,3			■	■	
	Read & Retell 1,2,3				■	■
	Reading Sense 1,2,3					■
	Reading Clue 1,2,3					■
	The Basic Way 1,2,3					
	Read to Reach 1,2,3					
	The Best Way 1,2,3					
	Reading Source 1,2,3					
	Reading Peak 1,2,3					
	Read Up 1,2,3					
Curriculum Integration Reading Program	Subject Link Starter 1,2,3					■
	Subject Link 1,2,3					
	Subject Link 4,5,6					
	Subject Link 7,8,9					
Listening	Listening Seed 1,2,3			■	■	
	Listening Season 1,2,3					■
	Listening Planner 1,2,3					
Grammar	Grammar Space Kids 1,2,3			■	■	
	Grammar Space Beginner 1,2,3					■
	Grammar Space 1,2,3					
	Grammar in Mind 1,2,3					■
	Grammar in Focus 1,2,3					
	Grammar Effect 1,2,3					
Writing	Write Right Beginner 1,2,3				■	■
	Write Right 1,2,3					
	Write Right Paragraph to Essay 1,2,3					
Speaking	Everyone, Speak! Kids 1,2,3			■		
	Everyone, Speak! Beginner 1,2,3				■	■
	Everyone, Speak! 1,2,3					

WORKBOOK

Reading Peak 3

NE_Build & Grow

WORKBOOK

Reading Peak 3

NE_Build & Grow

Unit 01 A Fairy Tale

Vocabulary Practice

A. Write the best word for each sentence. Change its form if necessary.

scary nightmare introduce tale stomach

1. Hunger is making my ______________ growl.
2. I'd like to ______________ a new company product.
3. The movie is so ______________ that it must not be shown to children.
4. Robert told us fantastic ______________ from his trip to Spain.
5. I woke up screaming in the middle of the night, after a(n) ______________.

B. Choose the best word for each blank.

1. Fire fighters and doctors work hard to ______________ people's lives.
   a. harm b. save c. expand d. interview
2. The storm is so ______________ that we must stay inside.
   a. violent b. famous c. magical d. religious
3. The movie is different from the ______________ story.
   a. sick b. safe c. useful d. original
4. The singer created several ______________ of his hit song for his fans.
   a. jackets b. versions c. endings d. characters
5. Melanie spent many years studying literature and became a(n) ______________.
   a. reader b. consumer c. scholar d. magician

C. Write the best phrase for each sentence. Change its form if necessary.

in fact translate ... into that's why

1. I didn't fail the exam; ______________ I did rather well.
2. Mia is a warm and caring person. ______________ people like her.
3. I need a person who can ______________ this article ______________ Spanish.

Writing Practice

A. Change the sentences as in the example.

Ex People have changed the stories in order to be told to children.
→ People have changed the stories **so that** they **can** be told to children.

1. I booked the ticket two weeks in advance in order to get a discount.
→ ______________________________

2. Brandon sometimes listens to classical music in order to broaden his views.
→ ______________________________

3. Please raise your hand first in order to have a chance to answer the question.
→ ______________________________

B. Match the sentence parts.

1. A hunter saves them •	• a. to be less scary.
2. People around the world translated •	• b. still enjoyed around the world.
3. *Sleeping Beauty* changed this character •	• c. who wanted to eat Sleeping Beauty.
4. The fairy Maleficent was an ogre •	• d. by cutting open the wolf's stomach.
5. The stories of the Brothers Grimm are •	• e. them into more than 160 languages.

C. Make the sentences with the given words and write them.

1. (violent / The original / more / even / was / story).
→ ______________________________

2. (wanted / They / to / their stories / introduce / German culture / through).
→ ______________________________

3. (these stories / to / sleep / going / read / Many children / before).
→ ______________________________

4. (fairy tales / are / That's / too frightening / usually / not / why).
→ ______________________________

5. (by / It / two brothers, / written / Jacob and Wilhelm Grimm / was).
→ ______________________________

Unit 02

Fair Trade

Vocabulary Practice

A. Write the best word for each sentence. Change its form if necessary.

extra　involve　purchase　raise　rare

1. I don't want to be ______________ in this problem.
2. We could stay there one more night at no ______________ cost.
3. I moved to a new house and ______________ new furniture.
4. Hotels usually ______________ their prices in the high season.
5. The ring that Sue is wearing is very unique and ______________.

B. Choose the best word for each blank.

1. This ______________ is a display model, so it's not for sale.
   a. item　b. trade　c. opinion　d. theory
2. Mike ______________ enough to feed his family.
   a. keeps　b. earns　c. causes　d. happens
3. If you ______________ to the plan, please raise your hand.
   a. sell　b. agree　c. include　d. frighten
4. We will give you a(n) ______________ discount if you pay in cash.
   a. rare　b. safe　c. original　d. additional
5. My parents ______________ me to express my true feelings.
   a. pay　b. afford　c. produce　d. encourage

C. Write the best phrase for each sentence. Change its form if necessary.

make sure　in the long run　make a difference

1. I hope to do something that ______________.
2. Angela ______________ that she is never late for meetings.
3. I am sure that the new policy will work ______________.

Writing Practice

A. Change the sentences as in the example.

Ex They keep this additional money instead of giving it to the workers.
→ They do **not** give this additional money to the workers **but** keep it.

1. Amy bought a pink bicycle instead of green.
→ ____________________

2. I took a bus instead of a train.
→ ____________________

3. I put sugar on my fried chicken instead of salt.
→ ____________________

B. Match the sentence parts.

1. I want to make a difference • • a. to make more of certain items.
2. Fair trade makes sure • • b. who always buys fair trade products.
3. If there is too much of a product • • c. that workers earn a good salary.
4. Fair trade encourages workers • • d. in the lives of poor people.
5. We're talking to Ashley • • e. the price goes down.

C. Make the sentences with the given words and write them.

1. (I / a fair price / that / paid / workers / should / agree / be).
→ ____________________

2. (isn't / happens / anymore / the item / because / rare / This).
→ ____________________

3. (the extra money / to / workers / pay / afford / We / with / can).
→ ____________________

4. (for / fair trade items / know / will / Stores / pay / that / more / people).
→ ____________________

5. (usually / When / goods, / involved / are / trading / extra companies / there).
→ ____________________

Unit 03

Claude Monet

Vocabulary Practice

A. Write the best word for each sentence. Change its form if necessary.

term	focus	exactly	capture	positive

1. This research ______________ on the importance of regular exercise.
2. The ______________ was named after the person who discovered it.
3. Nobody remembered ______________ what the boss asked us.
4. I like books with a(n) ______________ message.
5. This picture ______________ the motion of people completely.

B. Choose the best word for each blank.

1. These days the colleges are in a festive ______________.
   a. mood b. game c. human d. picture
2. The theory is too ______________ to understand clearly.
   a. generous b. abstract c. realistic d. well-known
3. I decided to jog every morning to ______________ weight.
   a. lose b. create c. behave d. prepare
4. After ______________ the roads, more people will ride bicycles.
   a. paving b. saving c. painting d. packaging
5. The ______________ of the lecture is the ecosystem.
   a. object b. reject c. subject d. style

C. Write the best phrase for each sentence. Change its form if necessary.

laugh at	rather than	over and over

1. Sara made the same mistakes ______________.
2. I want us to be friends ______________ rivals.
3. You should not ______________ a person who falls down.

Writing Practice

A. Change the sentences as in the example.

Ex They began to see. How can light be beautiful?

→ They began to see how light can be beautiful?

1. I don't know. What should I do?

→ ______________________

2. Tell me. How could you make it?

→ ______________________

3. I want to know. When will you come back?

→ ______________________

B. Match the sentence parts.

1. Monet started to focus •	• a. people laughed at it.
2. When he first showed it, •	• b. on light and color.
3. He would paint one object •	• c. how light can be beautiful.
4. They soon began to see •	• d. but no two are exactly the same.
5. Many of them look alike, •	• e. over and over at different times.

C. Make the sentences with the given words and write them.

1. (paintings / People / thought / look / should / reality / like).

→ ______________________

2. (used / A journalist / the term / a joke / as).

→ ______________________

3. (He / in / painted / various colors / types of light / and / them).

→ ______________________

4. (Modern painters / the freedom / to / what / they / feel / have / paint).

→ ______________________

5. (Monet / emotion / on / than / rather / focused / realism).

→ ______________________

Shark Fins

Vocabulary Practice

A. Write the best word for each sentence. Change its form if necessary.

prey enforce cruel throw official

1. It is ______________ to hunt animals for fun.
2. The pitcher ______________ the ball so hard that it went over the fence.
3. You need to pass a special exam to be a government ______________.
4. Wild birds often die of hunger because of the lack of ______________.
5. Police will begin to ______________ the new bike helmet law from July 1.

B. Choose the best word for each blank.

1. I'd like to try the restaurant's ______________.
   a. penalty b. demand c. loyalty d. specialty
2. The list of ______________ sounds very appetizing.
   a. rules b. laws c. oceans d. ingredients
3. Angelina lost her ______________, and fell on her behind.
   a. balance b. volume c. height d. manner
4. Being stuck in an elevator was a(n) ______________ experience.
   a. increasing b. releasing c. terrifying d. monitoring
5. Scientists have many theories about the ______________ of dinosaurs.
   a. practice b. extinction c. ecosystem d. ingredient

C. Write the best phrase for each sentence. Change its form if necessary.

in danger of at least not ... but~

1. I wash my car ______________ once a week.
2. I did ______________ major in literature ______________ in physics.
3. Don't forget that you're ______________ failing this course.

Writing Practice

A. Change the sentences as in the example.

Ex It is a very cruel and wasteful practice.
→ **What** a cruel and wasteful practice it is!

1. It was a very colorful and lively doll.
→ ______________________________

2. You have a very good sense of humor.
→ ______________________________

3. We are living in a very wonderful world.
→ ______________________________

B. Match the sentence parts.

1. Many people think of sharks • • a. of the food chain in the ocean.
2. New laws should be created so that • • b. that are already in place.
3. As demand for shark fin soup rises, • • c. countries can work together.
4. Sharks are at the top • • d. as terrifying animals.
5. Officials should enforce the fishing laws • • e. sharks are increasingly in danger.

C. Make the sentences with the given words and write them.

1. (very / to / are / Sharks / important / balance / the ecosystem's).
→ ______________________________

2. (some people / may / It / you / that / to / eat / surprise / know / them)
→ ______________________________

3. (More / are / it / eating / more / people / and / these days).
→ ______________________________

4. (A ban / for / would / on / decrease / sharks' fins / demand / shark fin soup).
→ ______________________________

5. (too many / smaller fish / there / would / Without / sharks, / be).
→ ______________________________

Unit 05

Nomadic People

Vocabulary Practice

A. Write the best word for each sentence. Change its form if necessary.

possession harsh boil consider grassland

1. Add noodles to the ______________ water and stir it.
2. Why do you ______________ the report false?
3. When you travel, you should be careful to keep your ______________ safe.
4. I see hundreds of sheep running on the ______________.
5. The tree survived the ______________ winter and blossomed in the spring.

B. Choose the best word for each blank.

1. Smoke from cars is ______________ our health.
   a. owning b. moving c. respecting d. threatening
2. I want to ______________ a good relationship with you.
   a. hunt b. hurt c. dash d. maintain
3. This place is ______________ for using public transportation.
   a. plain b. local c. fertile d. convenient
4. The cave provided a(n) ______________ from the hurricane.
   a. shelter b. vision c. outdoor d. activity
5. I'll change my computer because it is ______________.
   a. dateless b. fertile c. up-to-date d. outdated

C. Write the best phrase for each sentence. Change its form if necessary.

such as consist of take advantage of

1. You should be sure to ______________ this chance.
2. This cookie ______________ egg whites and sugar only.
3. I enjoy water sports, ______________ surfing and snorkeling.

Writing Practice

A. Change the sentences as in the example.

Ex To respect and maintain every way of life is important.
→ It is important to respect and maintain every way of life.

1. To point out a person's mistakes is easy.
   → ______________________________
2. To make others understand me fully is difficult.
   → ______________________________
3. To create sounds with wind instruments is not easy.
   → ______________________________

B. Match the sentence parts.

1. Almost everyone lives • • a. who have special homes.
2. They consider the mountains • • b. in some kind of shelter.
3. To grow crops, • • c. to cook food and boil water.
4. Dried yak dung is used • • d. Tibetan nomads use fertile land.
5. There are some people • • e. their home.

C. Make the sentences with the given words and write them.

1. (harsh / them / Yak skin / from / weather / protects).
   → ______________________________
2. (them / to / They / of / take / survive / full advantage).
   → ______________________________
3. (another place / the soil / turns / They / to / before / go / bad).
   → ______________________________
4. (wool / Tibetan / make / yak / tents / nomads / from).
   → ______________________________
5. (by / threatened / of / Tibetan nomads / is / The lifestyle / being / big cities).
   → ______________________________

Unit 06 Constellations

Vocabulary Practice

A. Write the best word for each sentence. Change its form if necessary.

approach tough hunt drip bleed

1. You need a license to ______________ in this area.
2. The athlete was so ______________ that he played even though he was injured.
3. Hallie is a very cold person and is difficult to ______________.
4. Turn the faucet tight so that the water doesn't ______________.
5. If you get many nose ______________, you should go see a doctor.

B. Choose the best word for each blank.

1. On the bus, Tim ______________ that he didn't bring Amy's birthday present.
   a. chased b. realized c. decided d. terrorized
2. There still are uncivilized ______________ in the jungle.
   a. tribes b. patterns c. abilities d. horizon
3. Children's favorite ______________ is playing with their friends.
   a. village b. pastime c. attraction d. constellation
4. Susan was too ______________ to scream for help or to move her legs.
   a. vicious b. pleased c. terrified d. satisfied
5. Luke ______________ the criminal, but he couldn't catch him.
   a. boiled b. issued c. pursued d. consumed

C. Write the best phrase for each sentence. Change its form if necessary.

be known as run away pick out

1. The horse jumped over the fence and ______________.
2. Norma Jeane ______________ Marilyn Monroe.
3. My mother helped me ______________ an outfit to wear to the party.

Writing Practice

A. Change the sentences as in the example.

Ex The bear was very terrified, so he ray away.
➡ The bear was **so** terrified **that** he ran away.

1. Josh was very angry, so his face turned red.
➡ ______________________________

2. Mike ran very fast, so I couldn't catch him.
➡ ______________________________

3. Ashley was very wise, so she could deal with the problem.
➡ ______________________________

B. Match the sentence parts.

1. The stars form a shape similar •
2. He ran into the sky •
3. The warriors chased him •
4. His favorite pastime was •
5. The three warriors were •

• a. to escape the warriors.
• b. attacking villages and people.
• c. to a big bear.
• d. very tough and courageous.
• e. for months and months.

C. Make the sentences with the given words and write them.

1. (a group / for / called / They / stars / looked / of / the Big Dipper).
➡ ______________________________

2. (didn't / He / to / him / expect / pursue / them)!
➡ ______________________________

3. (the bear / One / an arrow / the warriors / of / shot / with).
➡ ______________________________

4. (very vicious / was / says / was / The story / an enormous bear / that / there).
➡ ______________________________

5. (the bear / When / his blood / drips / the Earth / the horizon, / approaches / onto).
➡ ______________________________

Unit 07 LOHAS

Vocabulary Practice

A. Write the best word for each sentence. Change its form if necessary.

packaging   distance   rapidly   well-being   resource

1. The excitement made my heart beat ________________.
2. Please measure the ________________ from here to that point.
3. Because of poor ________________, the products were damaged.
4. This company tries to find ways to protect natural ________________.
5. Skipping breakfast can affect learning, memory, and physical ________________.

B. Choose the best word for each blank.

1. The ________________ in big cities is usually polluted.
   a. evolution   b. enthusiasm   c. environment   d. organization
2. This vehicle is used to ________________ goods.
   a. join   b. support   c. describe   d. transport
3. I helped my father spray crops with ________________.
   a. benefits   b. companies   c. consumers   d. pesticides
4. Your question had no ________________ connection with our discussion.
   a. scary   b. direct   c. organic   d. distant
5. Environmental ________________ became an important issue in the industry.
   a. disability   b. capability   c. personality   d. sustainability

C. Write the best phrase for each sentence. Change its form if necessary.

stand for   focus on   care about

1. A flag ________________ the country and its citizens.
2. Sean doesn't ________________ anything but himself.
3. The company ________________ the development of cellular phone technology.

Writing Practice

A. Change the sentences as in the example.

Ex Do you care about your health and the environment?
→ Do you care about **not only** your health **but also** the environment.

1. James writes children's books and adults' books.
→ ______________________________

2. I enjoy reading books and doing outdoor activities.
→ ______________________________

3. Physical education strengthens students' bodies and minds.
→ ______________________________

B. Match the sentence parts.

1. LOHAS members focus on • • a. free from harmful chemicals.
2. LOHAS is a term • • b. to join their movement.
3. Organic food is grown • • c. without pesticides.
4. LOHAS members want consumers • • d. buying local food.
5. It helps keep our water supply • • e. that describes a certain type of consumer.

C. Make the sentences with the given words and write them.

1. (They / everyone / care / the environment / that / hope / will / about).
→ ______________________________

2. (not / shipped / be / distances / have / Local food / does / long / to).
→ ______________________________

3. (when / transporting / is / it / Less / fuel / used).
→ ______________________________

4. (to / It / not / is / oil / sustainable / use / continue / so much / to).
→ ______________________________

5. (to / the environment / The mission / is / about / encourage / to / consumers / care).
→ ______________________________

The Secret Garden

Vocabulary Practice

A. Write the best word for each sentence. Change its form if necessary.

delighted complain return maid nurse

1. I ______________ the plant along for a year.
2. Rebecca was ______________ to hear the good news.
3. My aunt needs three more ______________ to help prepare for the party.
4. Nobody knows how to ______________ to where they started their journey.
5. Customers who ______________ are helpful for companies to grow.

B. Choose the best word for each blank.

1. It is a blessing to forget ______________ memories.
   a. favorite b. positive c. unreliable d. unpleasant
2. Jessica ______________ ate any of the cake because she was full.
   a. really b. solely c. barely d. luckily
3. If you are ______________ to others, then people will act the same to you.
   a. rude b. nude c. loud d. rare
4. My mother has a special ______________ recipe.
   a. call b. secret c. change d. message
5. Eric tried to ______________ all the difficulties to succeed.
   a. nurse b. decide c. bear d. discover

C. Write the best phrase for each sentence. Change its form if necessary.

thanks to at first used to

1. I ______________ play in the attic when I was young.
2. Mike could be safe from the accident ______________ his seatbelt.
3. ______________, Anne worked as a professor but later became an actress.

Writing Practice

A. Change the sentences as in the example.

Ex Martha tells about a hidden garden. It used to be Mrs. Craven's favorite spot.
→ Martha tells about a hidden garden **that** used to be Mrs. Craven's favorite spot.

1. My grandmother gave me a piano. It had been played by her.
→ ______________________________

2. I watched the soccer match. It was one of the most exciting games.
→ ______________________________

3. I've studied hard for the test. It is important for me to pass.
→ ______________________________

B. Match the sentence parts.

1. As the garden grows,	•	•	a. and to think positively.
2. It remains a children's favorite	•	•	b. Mary becomes happier.
3. They learn to care about others	•	•	c. to see that his son can walk.
4. She slowly nurses	•	•	d. because of its fascinating story.
5. He is delighted	•	•	e. the garden back to life.

C. Make the sentences with the given words and write them.

1. (her / named / A maid / spends / time / Martha / with).
→ ______________________________

2. (becomes / with / Colin, / friends / Mary / Mr. Craven's son).
→ ______________________________

3. (to / live / in / she / He / be / bear / the house / in / to / used / can't).
→ ______________________________

4. (something / With / they / are / grow / into / beautiful / to / a little love / able).
→ ______________________________

5. (make / Mary / project / decides / special / it / to / her).
→ ______________________________

Unit 09

Bacteria Vs. Viruses

Vocabulary Practice

A. Write the best word for each sentence. Change its form if necessary.

prevent frequently medication spread contact

1. The police are trying to ______________ crimes.
2. Take the ______________ three times a day after meals.
3. I have not had any ______________ with her for a very long time.
4. I ______________ visit the restaurant and I like its food.
5. The rumor about Cindy quickly ______________ through the town.

B. Choose the best word for each blank.

1. Cheese is very ______________ but high in calories.
   a. nutritious b. harmful c. pleasant d. similar
2. You can use the bank's safety box to store your ______________ things.
   a. negative b. valuable c. common d. impossible
3. My parents had a lot of ______________ and gave me endless support.
   a. haste b. patience c. fluids d. medication
4. I hope we can ______________ ideas during the meeting.
   a. avoid b. exist c. disappear d. exchange
5. Tim had to stay alone in his room to prevent ______________ from outside.
   a. vitamin b. benefit c. infection d. nature

C. Write the best phrase for each sentence. Change its form if necessary.

stay away from plenty of lead to

1. Eating too much fat can ______________ high blood cholesterol.
2. Lauren has retired and she has ______________ free time.
3. Leave him alone because he prefers to ______________ others.

Writing Practice

A. Change the sentences as in the example.

Ex There are differences between the two, but the way they spread is similar.
→ **Though** there are differences between the two, the way they spread is similar.

1. Sam tried to meet Henry several times, but he failed.
→ ______________________________

2. I studied very hard for the exam, but I couldn't pass it.
→ ______________________________

3. Everyone expected that we would win the first prize, but we couldn't reach the finals.
→ ______________________________

B. Match the sentence parts.

1. We can be infected •
2. Viruses are found •
3. We're usually told to stay away •
4. If we do interact with them, •
5. Their benefits outweigh •

• a. their bad effects.
• b. through coughing and sneezing.
• c. we should wash our hands frequently.
• d. wherever there is life.
• e. from places with bacteria.

C. Make the sentences with the given words and write them.

1. (made / by / oxygen / Almost 50% / is / bacteria / of).
→ ______________________________

2. (create / as / vitamin K / help / such / They / valuable vitamins).
→ ______________________________

3. (is / It / live / without / impossible / almost / to / bacteria).
→ ______________________________

4. (should / remain / we / sick / contact / To / avoid / with / healthy, / people).
→ ______________________________

5. (like / made / yogurt and cheese / without / cannot / Nutritious foods / be / bacteria).
→ ______________________________

Unit 10

Mardi Gras

Vocabulary Practice

A. Write the best word for each sentence. Change its form if necessary.

unique   last   experience   celebration   enormous

1. You need to ______________ various types of social life.
2. Jim is quite ______________ compared to most people I know.
3. Rebecca is very rich and she lives in a(n) ______________ mansion.
4. I hope this excellent weather will ______________ until this weekend.
5. I held a 60th wedding anniversary ______________ for my parents.

B. Choose the best word for each blank.

1. The beautiful sceneries are one of the ______________ of Switzerland.
   a. infections   b. attractions   c. interactions   d. nutrition
2. James and his boss rushed to the airport so not to ______________ the flight.
   a. miss   b. visit   c. attend   d. organize
3. At the party, I am going to wear a king's ______________.
   a. coins   b. floats   c. costume   d. audience
4. The cafe was ______________ used as a guest house 10 years ago.
   a. originally   b. creatively   c. fortunately   d. enormously
5. The schools closed for the long ______________ weekend.
   a. ball   b. beads   c. nation   d. holiday

C. Write the best phrase for each sentence. Change its form if necessary.

enjoy oneself   a great deal of   give up

1. I ______________ to the fullest in Hawaii last summer.
2. Jackson's song brought him ______________ popularity.
3. Don't ______________ your dream because of your difficult situation.

Writing Practice

A. Change the sentences as in the example.

Ex You should not miss the main attraction.

➡ Be sure **not to miss** the main attraction.

1. You should not speak ill of your friends.

➡ ______________________________

2. You should not forget to show gratitude to your parents.

➡ ______________________________

3. You should not avoid hardship before trying to overcome it.

➡ ______________________________

B. Match the sentence parts.

1. The idea behind Mardi Gras was •	• a. to a ball.
2. Mardi Gras celebrations last •	• b. for two weeks.
3. You might even be invited •	• c. by a group or "krewe."
4. Mardi Gras is one of •	• d. to eat and party before Lent.
5. Each parade is organized •	• e. the best festivals in the world.

C. Make the sentences with the given words and write them.

1. (until / You / are / can / you / stuffed / eat).

➡ ______________________________

2. (yourself / to / You / enjoy / of / have / time / a great deal).

➡ ______________________________

3. (during / might / One thing / Mardi Gras / is / you / king cake / eat).

➡ ______________________________

4. (to / festival / brought / the United States / this / The French).

➡ ______________________________

5. (such / certain foods / You / as / must / up / enjoyable things, / give / eating).

➡ ______________________________

Unit 11

Maps

Vocabulary Practice

A. Write the best word for each sentence. Change its form if necessary.

entire   satellite   wonder   revolution   transport

1. I ______________ if I can get the money back.
2. The products are going to be ______________ by airplane.
3. The ______________ was launched in a rocket.
4. The invention of electricity was a(n) ______________ for humans.
5. Julie donated her ______________ savings to poor students.

B. Choose the best word for each blank.

1. The Wright brothers ______________ the airplane.
   a. ruined   b. carved   c. invented   d. destroyed
2. You need to take another ______________ to get there sooner.
   a. action   b. place   c. route   d. pattern
3. In the near future, commom people could ______________ space.
   a. explore   b. include   c. escape   d. express
4. Even if the society ______________, it doesn't mean it becomes better for everyone.
   a. updates   b. produces   c. advertises   d. advances
5. New technologies have made our life more ______________ in some ways.
   a. exact   b. expensive   c. convenient   d. outdated

C. Write the best phrase for each sentence. Change its form if necessary.

look like   in order to   piece by piece

1. You ______________ a totally different person.
2. I worked very hard ______________ make the world better.
3. The detective looked through the letters ______________ for clues.

Writing Practice

A. Change the sentences as in the example.

Ex You only have to go online.
→ **All** you have to do **is to go** online.

1. We only had to wait for the snow to stop.
→ ______________________________

2. You only have to fill in this form.
→ ______________________________

3. You only have to listen to what your friends say.
→ ______________________________

B. Match the sentence parts.

1. People didn't know •	• a. to print their maps on paper.
2. We have gone from stone tablets •	• b. what the world looked like.
3. As people traveled further, •	• c. to complex digital maps.
4. Mapmakers were able •	• d. that show us exactly where we are.
5. There are navigation maps •	• e. they were able to update the maps.

C. Make the sentences with the given words and write them.

1. (develop / continue / detailed and convenient / We / to / more / maps).
→ ______________________________

2. (complex / often / to / make / use / technology / maps / We).
→ ______________________________

3. (that / was / showed / 1507 / made / the whole world / in / The first map).
→ ______________________________

4. (As / use / the way / we / is / maps / advances, / changing / technology).
→ ______________________________

5. (Satellite maps / what / from / show / look / places / us / the sky / like).
→ ______________________________

Unit 12 Rosa Parks

Vocabulary Practice

A. Write the best word for each sentence. Change its form if necessary.

secretary abandon treatment bold significant

1. The thieves ______________ the car on the road.
2. The most ______________ issue today is the energy problem.
3. Angela was ______________ enough to walk by herself at night.
4. We're trying to give all the members better ______________.
5. Please leave a message with my ______________, in case of my absence.

B. Choose the best word for each blank.

1. There is ______________ between the rich and the poor.
   a. racism b. symbol c. education d. inequality
2. It's time to ______________ the plane now.
   a. cause b. involve c. board d. prevent
3. I have a lot of work to do, so I have to ______________ your invitation.
   a. fight b. refuse c. confuse d. invent
4. I have a strong ______________ that I will succeed.
   a. act b. right c. section d. belief
5. Police entered the store to ______________ the criminals who stole the CDs.
   a. arrest b. ride c. spark d. divide

C. Write the best phrase for each sentence. Change its form if necessary.

stand up for be regarded as in spite of

1. Daniel ______________ on of our top reporters.
2. Women are ______________ their rights.
3. ______________ my warning, Emma still wants to go there.

Writing Practice

A. Change the sentences as in the example.

Ex Rose watched her white classmates. They rode on a different section of the bus.
→ Rose **watched her white classmates ride** on a different section of the bus.

1. Christina felt something. It moved behind her.
→ ______________________________

2. My dog heard a bee. It buzzed around him.
→ ______________________________

3. The police officer saw a man. He crossed the street against a red light.
→ ______________________________

B. Match the sentence parts.

1. Rosa is regarded as •	• a. became even more significant.
2. Rosa's role in the movement •	• b. a symbol of the civil rights movement.
3. The driver told Rosa •	• c. against black people at that time.
4. There was a lot of racism •	• d. in the fight against inequality.
5. Rosa became actively involved •	• e. to abandon her seat.

C. Make the sentences with the given words and write them.

1. (as / She / against / a fighter / regarded / racial inequality / is).
→ ______________________________

2. (arrested / called / and / The driver / she / the police / was).
→ ______________________________

3. (the unfair treatment / society / Her courage / blacks / of / showed).
→ ______________________________

4. (Blacks and whites / on / into / sections / were / buses / divided / different).
→ ______________________________

5. (This single act / the movement / of / sparked / the beginning / by / Rosa Parks).
→ ______________________________

Unit 13 Reptiles

Vocabulary Practice

A. Write the best word for each sentence. Change its form if necessary.

unfriendly mammal villain independent species

1. Whales are ________________, not fish.
2. My younger sister is very ________________ even though she's young.
3. James often plays the part of the ________________, not the hero.
4. There are 5,000 different ________________ of seaweed.
5. The staff at the restaurant was ________________ and made mistakes.

B. Choose the best word for each blank.

1. They built a high wall to prevent ________________ from attacking.
   a. capital b. audience c. features d. enemies
2. When I stroke ________________ animals like cats, I feel relieved.
   a. dairy b. scary c. furry d. afraid
3. It was a ________________ belief once that the Earth was flat.
   a. scaly b. close c. unique d. common
4. Humans can't ________________ climate changes.
   a. hide b. stuff c. regard d. control
5. How did Emily ________________ to the news?
   a. include b. respect c. respond d. explore

C. Write the best phrase for each sentence. Change its form if necessary.

as soon as even though according to

1. Prices of these tables vary ________________ size.
2. I can't go to my hometown ________________ it's very close.
3. Tickets for the concert sold out ________________ they were released.

Writing Practice

A. Change the sentences as in the example.

Ex Turtles are fast reptiles. (in the world)

→ Turtles are **the fastest reptiles** in the world.

1. The golfer is young to win. (the world championship)

   → ____________________

2. This is a cheap flight ticket to Manila. (during peak season)

   → ____________________

3. This fast food restaurant sells large hamburgers. (in the city)

   → ____________________

B. Match the sentence parts.

1. Are you afraid •	• a. to outside temperatures.
2. Chameleons are known •	• b. because they aren't furry?
3. Do reptiles seem unfriendly •	• c. to hide from enemies.
4. Chameleons respond •	• d. of reptiles?
5. Changing their color helps them •	• e. to be particularly interesting.

C. Make the sentences with the given words and write them.

1. (away / scaly skin / turn / Don't / because / of / their).

   → ____________________

2. (in / Antarctica / except / They / found / continent / every / can / be).

   → ____________________

3. (in / the sun / That's / lay / up / to / why / warm / many / reptiles).

   → ____________________

4. (see / on / the ground, / don't / you / a snake / run / away / Next time).

   → ____________________

5. (out / of / are / as soon as / independent / they / their shells / Their babies / break).

   → ____________________

Unit 14

Science Fiction

Vocabulary Practice

A. Write the best word for each sentence. Change its form if necessary.

major   kidnap   feature   humanity   distant

1. My school days are really ______________ memories.
2. Advanced technology might destroy ______________.
3. That Christmas movie ______________ a wise boy and stupid thieves.
4. Teenagers' ______________ concerns are related to their friends.
5. The criminal who ______________ the child was arrested by the police.

B. Choose the best word for each blank.

1. I'd like to ______________ a question about the fees.
   a. raise   b. imagine   c. discover   d. interest
2. Car accidents ______________ a lot near this intersection.
   a. bring   b. happen   c. destroy   d. consume
3. Astronomers search the ______________ for new stars.
   a. sea   b. effect   c. reality   d. universe
4. Nobody wants to be ______________ by other people.
   a. praised   b. allowed   c. controlled   d. imagined
5. The ______________ of the printing press caused a huge increase in literacy.
   a. fiction   b. genre   c. invention   d. relationship

C. Write the best phrase for each sentence. Change its form if necessary.

even if   go through   appeal to

1. Please be understanding ______________ I make a mistake.
2. Tom seems to know how to ______________ women.
3. Our team ______________ hard training to prepare for the game.

Writing Practice

A. Change the sentences as in the example.

Ex Why is science fiction such a major genre?
→ It's easy to see **why** science fiction is such a major genre.

1. How does the machine work in this severe weather?
→ I want to know ______________________

2. When is the train going to depart Central Station for Chicago?
→ We will announce ______________________

3. Why did the man hide the truth?
→ I don't know ______________________

B. Match the sentence parts.

1. Neo is kidnapped •
2. The world he knows is images •
3. The movie allows us to •
4. You can imagine •
5. You are given a chance •

• a. imagine a different world.
• b. to think about our world.
• c. machines that don't exist yet.
• d. created by computers.
• e. by a mysterious woman.

C. Make the sentences with the given words and write them.

1. (about / to / Science fiction / think / us / our world / stimulates).
→ ______________________

2. (our world / about / going / through / changes / that / is / are / The stories).
→ ______________________

3. (reality / by / machines / humans / are / is / controlled / that / The frightening).
→ ______________________

4. (what / to / like / exciting / imagine / be / our lives / would / It's).
→ ______________________

5. (about / They / to / raise / humanity's relationship / the universe / basic questions).
→ ______________________

Unit 15

Animal Defenses

Vocabulary Practice

A. Write the best word for each sentence. Change its form if necessary.

predator confuse involve smelly spray

1. Don't ______________ everyone else in this problem.
2. The water was ______________ from the hose.
3. I didn't eat the meat because it was ______________.
4. Teens like games so much that they ______________ fantasy and real life.
5. ______________ play an important role in the balance of the ecosystem.

B. Choose the best word for each blank.

1. My son had a hard time ______________ to his new school at first.
   a. chasing b. adapting c. affecting d. prompting
2. The police failed to ______________ the thieves.
   a. hide b. evolve c. escape d. capture
3. I don't like tiny ______________ that have a lot of legs and look gross.
   a. birds b. insects c. animals d. mammals
4. The children ______________ their toys all over the room.
   a. escaped b. attacked c. scattered d. defended
5. Some farmers use too many agricultural ______________ to grow fruits.
   a. spices b. chemicals c. artificials d. surroundings

C. Write the best phrase for each sentence. Change its form if necessary.

in packs be likely to blend in

1. I attended every town meeting to ______________ with the community.
2. Gypsies usually get along with each other and move ______________.
3. My mother ______________ visit your country this time.

Writing Practice

A. Change the sentences as in the example.

Ex You would probably hide. It is a basic way to escape predators.
→ You would probably hide, **which** is a basic way to escape predators.

1. Brad Pitt starred in the film *Interview with the Vampire*. It was made in 1994.
→ ______________________________
2. We train workers to be skillful. It is essential to our company.
→ ______________________________
3. The liquid soap is made of natural ingredients. It appeals to many people.
→ ______________________________

B. Match the sentence parts.

1. There are even insects •
2. The predator will have to •
3. They are able to blend in •
4. These methods of defense •
5. Skunks spray smelly chemicals •

• a. don't always work.
• b. at their predators.
• c. that look exactly like twigs.
• d. pick only one to chase after.
• e. with their surroundings.

C. Make the sentences with the given words and write them.

1. (defend / animals / ways / have / to / Many / unique / themselves).
→ ______________________________
2. (stay / way / be / is / to / in / a group / The easiest / to / safe).
→ ______________________________
3. (is / that's / more / alone / likely / to / A predator / an animal / attack).
→ ______________________________
4. (likely / If / be / attacks / to / caught / the group, / each individual / a predator / is / less).
→ ______________________________
5. (involves / the most / defense / chemicals / amazing / of / types / One of).
→ ______________________________

Unit 16

The Galápagos Islands

Vocabulary Practice

A. Write the best word for each sentence. Change its form if necessary.

central pollute restriction illegal native

1. It is ______________ to copy a book or CD.
2. The city hall is in the ______________ part of the town.
3. There is no ______________ on changing one's last name nowadays.
4. Some countries ______________ the environment for their economic growth.
5. Sam left his ______________ land and never returned.

B. Choose the best word for each blank.

1. There are a lot of ______________ that explain the symptoms.
   a. theories b. standards c. complaints d. predictions
2. That river is the natural ______________ of several species of fish.
   a. state b. group c. habitat d. country
3. There are laws that protect the ______________ in this park.
   a. origin b. region c. wildlife d. pollution
4. I don't listen to music when studying because it ______________ my concentration.
   a. forces b. disturbs c. disguises d. researches
5. Pollution is a serious ______________ to people's health.
   a. effort b. peak c. threat d. research

C. Write the best phrase for each sentence. Change its form if necessary.

get rid of bring in thanks to

1. The magic show ______________ a large crowd.
2. I try to ______________ stress by playing sports.
3. ______________ your help, I could get there in time.

Writing Practice

A. Change the sentences as in the example.

Ex You are not a scientist so you don't want to research the Galápagos Islands.
→ **If** you **were** a scientist, you **might want** to research the Galápagos Islands.

1. You are not a teacher so you don't worry about various teaching methods.
→ ______________________________

2. You are not a singer so you don't have to spend lots of time singing and dancing.
→ ______________________________

3. You are not a politician so you don't study how to get people's attention.
→ ______________________________

B. Match the sentence parts.

1. The islands are home •		• a. to his theory of evolution.
2. There are more foreign species •		• b. be on a list of endangered places.
3. The native species are often •		• c. not able to defend themselves.
4. The islands used to •		• d. to many rare plant and animal species.
5. His research there was central •		• e. than native species in the Galápagos.

C. Make the sentences with the given words and write them.

1. (many / Pirates / in / species / brought / non-native / have).
→ ______________________________

2. (able / You / to / plants and animals / be / see / will / unique).
→ ______________________________

3. (a big / These animals / species / threat / can / the native / be / to).
→ ______________________________

4. (Tourism / the plants and animals / people / dangerous / because / can / disturb / be).
→ ______________________________

5. (are / the islands / There / dangers / other / to / also).
→ ______________________________

Word List

Unit 01

- original
- violent
- scholar
- folk
- publish
- religious
- scary
- translate
- nightmare
- frightening

Unit 02

- fair
- opinion
- average
- afford
- extra
- involve
- earn
- additional
- encourage
- rare

Unit 03

- term
- subject
- exactly
- capture
- significance
- appearance
- emotion
- pave
- abstract
- freedom

Unit 04

- terrify
- practice
- prey
- demand
- extinction
- official
- enforce
- monitor
- ban
- ingredient

Unit 05

- shelter
- consider
- grassland
- possession
- harsh
- boil
- consist
- crop
- outdated
- respect

Unit 06

- enormous
- vicious
- tough

- courageous
- realize
- coward
- escape
- pursue
- approach
- drip

Unit 07

- organic
- describe
- consumer
- sustainability
- direct
- well-being
- mission
- offer
- distance
- pesticide

Unit 08

- orphan
- bear
- maid
- spot
- nurse
- barely
- return
- positive
- rude
- complain

Unit 09

- negative
- outweigh
- infection
- valuable
- medication
- patience
- disappear
- spread
- exchange
- contact

Unit 10

- holiday
- capital
- celebration
- last
- incredible
- stuff
- invite
- attraction
- organize
- experience

Unit 11

- wonder
- explore
- entire
- carve
- revolution
- transport
- complex

- satellite
- advance
- convenient

Unit 12

- divide
- inequality
- secretary
- abandon
- arrest
- bold
- spark
- unfair
- treatment
- regard

Unit13

- furry
- mammal
- feature
- continent
- species
- waterproof
- aquatic
- enemy
- reputation
- villain

Unit 14

- kidnap
- reality
- distant
- stimulate
- force
- major
- fancy
- raise
- humanity
- universe

Unit 15

- predator
- defend
- individual
- pack
- scatter
- direction
- adapt
- involve
- evolve
- spray

Unit 16

- wildlife
- theory
- evolution
- native
- attack
- habitat
- disturb
- pollute
- restriction
- remove

Aqua

Reading Peak Aqua is a three-level nonfiction reading series designed for intermediate to high intermediate students. Compelling topics motivate students and make reading exercises informative and meaningful. This series presents background knowledge passages to ensure a better understanding of topics while engaging the interest of readers. All readings are based on carefully considered word lists to expand students' vocabulary and develop their reading fluency. This series includes reading comprehension questions to enhance students' critical thinking skills. With *Reading Peak Aqua*, students are ready to become advanced readers.

Features:

- Engaging, academic nonfiction readings in various forms of writing
- Interesting, informative background knowledge
- Exercises to improve reading speed
- Open-ended questions that strengthen students' thinking and writing skills
- Basic reading strategies accompanied by simple exercises
- Level-appropriate word lists and definitions before each main reading
- Graphic organizers to support students' mind mapping abilities
- Workbook for more vocabulary, grammar, and writing practice

Components:

Student Book / Workbook / Audio CD

Online Resources: www.nebooks.co.kr (Korean) / www.nebuildandgrow.com (English)

MP3 files / Vocabulary lists / Answer keys and translations

Reading Peak Aqua Series:

[190~210 words]

[220~240 words]

[250~270 words]

Primary			Secondary			Components
Low Intermediate	Intermediate	High Intermediate	A	B	C	
						Student Book/ Workbook/ 2 MultiROMs
						Book/ Audio CD
						Student Book/ Workbook/ MultiROM
						Student Book/ Workbook/ Audio CD
						Student Book/ Workbook/ Audio CD
						Student Book/ Workbook/ Audio CD
						Student Book/ Workbook/ Audio CD
						Student Book/ Workbook/ Audio CD
						Student Book/ Workbook/ Audio CD
						Student Book/ Workbook/ Audio CD
						Student Book/ Workbook/ Audio CD
						Student Book/ Workbook/ Audio CD
						Student Book/ Workbook/ Audio CD
						Student Book/ Supplementary Material/ MP3 CD
						Student Book/ Workbook/ MultiROM
						Student Book/ Workbook/ Audio CD
						Student Book/ Workbook/ Audio CD
						Student Book/ Workbook/ Audio CD
						Student Book/ Workbook/ Scripts & Answer Keys/ Audio CD
						Student Book/ Workbook/ Scripts & Answer Keys/ MP3 CD
						Student Book/ Workbook/ Scripts & Answer Keys/ MP3 CD
						Student Book/ Workbook
						Student Book/ Workbook
						Student Book/ Workbook
						Student Book/ Workbook
						Student Book/ Workbook/ Audio CD
						Student Book/ Workbook/ Answer Keys
						Student Book/ Workbook
						Student Book/ Workbook
						Student Book/ Workbook
						Student Book/ Workbook/ MultiROM
						Student Book/ Workbook/ MultiROM
						Student Book/ Workbook/ MultiROM